Pro SQL Server on Microsoft Azure

T0215124

Pranab Mazumdar

Sourabh Agarwal

Amit Banerjee

Apress®

Pro SQL Server on Microsoft Azure

Pranab Mazumdar
Bangalore, Karnataka, India

Sourabh Agarwal
Bangalore, Karnataka, India

Amit Banerjee
Bangalore, Karnataka, India

ISBN-13 (pbk): 978-1-4842-2082-5
DOI 10.1007/978-1-4842-2083-2

ISBN-13 (electronic): 978-1-4842-2083-2

Library of Congress Control Number: 2016949375

Managing Director: Welmoed Spahr
Lead Editor: Celestin Suresh John
Technical Reviewer: Ravikanth Chaganti
Editorial Board: Steve Anglin, Pramila Balan, Laura Berendson, Aaron Black, Louise Corrigan,
    Jonathan Gennick, Robert Hutchinson, Celestin Suresh John, Nikhil Karkal,
    James Markham, Susan McDermott, Matthew Moodie, Natalie Pao, Gwenan Spearing
Coordinating Editor: Prachi Mehta
Copy Editor: Kezia Endsley
Compositor: SPi Global
Indexer: SPi Global
Artist: SPi Global

Distributed to the book trade worldwide by Springer Science+Business Media New York, 233 Spring Street, 6th Floor, New York, NY 10013. Phone 1-800-SPRINGER, fax (201) 348-4505, e-mail orders-ny@springer-sbm.com, or visit www.springeronline.com. Apress Media, LLC is a California LLC and the sole member (owner) is Springer Science + Business Media Finance Inc (SSBM Finance Inc). SSBM Finance Inc is a **Delaware** corporation.

For information on translations, please e-mail rights@apress.com, or visit www.apress.com.

Apress and friends of ED books may be purchased in bulk for academic, corporate, or promotional use. eBook versions and licenses are also available for most titles. For more information, reference our Special Bulk Sales–eBook Licensing web page at www.apress.com/bulk-sales.

Any source code or other supplementary materials referenced by the author in this text are available to readers at www.apress.com. For detailed information about how to locate your book's source code, go to www.apress.com/source-code/. Readers can also access source code at SpringerLink in the Supplementary Material section for each chapter.

Printed on acid-free paper

Contents at a Glance

Contents

About the Authors

Pranab Mazumdar is currently working as an Escalation Engineer for the Microsoft Azure SQL Database and Azure SQL Data Warehouse. He will soon be an Embedded Escalation Engineer, working very closely and partnering with the Engineering team. Prior to aligning to the cloud side of the business, he was an Escalation Engineer with the SQL Server team in CSS/GBS, where he worked with the product team to fix bugs in the SQL Server product, thereby making SQL a better and preferred RDBMS. He has been working with Microsoft for close to 12 years, with specializations in SQL Server Engine performance, high availability, and disaster recovery. He has worked with many large corporations with very large and complex SQL deployments.

Apart from SQL, he also worked with operational Insight, formerly known as System Centre Advisor, migrating and helping create new sets of rules and validation processes. He holds a number of Microsoft certifications, including MCAD, MCSD, MCDBA, MSCE, MCTS, MCITP, and MCT. The latest one is his Azure certification. He likes to be connected to his customers and he has been a speaker at TechEd, GIDs, SQL Saturday, SQL Talks, and other community UG events.

Sourabh Agarwal currently works as a Senior Premier Field Engineer for the Microsoft Enterprise Services Delivery team. During his decade-long stint at Microsoft, he has worked in different capacities and specializes in providing reactive and proactive consulting on SQL Server and related technologies to Microsoft Enterprise customers across business domains and geographies. His specializations include SQL Database Design, SQL Server performance optimization, HADR, Microsoft Azure, PowerShell Scripting, and Dimension Modeling/Data Warehouse designing.

Amit Banerjee currently works as a Senior Program Manager for the Microsoft SQL Server Product Group (Tiger Team). He has a decade of experience with SQL Server-related environments. Prior to this role, he worked as a Senior Premier Field Engineer at Microsoft, specializing in proactive and advisory assistance for SQL Server environments. In the past, he worked for the SQL Server Support team in various capacities, including the Microsoft SQL Server Escalation Services team. This involved fixing/troubleshooting complex issues related to SQL Server over a varied range of environments, including deployments handling from 100 to 10 million users. He worked on SQL Server environments for leading corporations in various business domains by helping them address and rectify SQL related issues for mission- and business-critical applications. He has also contributed to various related tools, including SQL Nexus, SQL Server Backup Simulator, and SQLDIAG/PSSDIAG Configuration Manager and is also the co-author of *Professional SQL Server 2012: Internals and Troubleshooting,* published by Wrox Press.

About the Technical Reviewer

Ravikanth is a Principal Engineer and the Lead Architect for Microsoft and VMware private and hybrid cloud solutions in the Enterprise Solutions Group at Dell Inc. He is a multi-year recipient of Microsoft's Most Valuable Professional (MVP) award in Windows PowerShell. Ravikanth is the author of *Windows PowerShell Desired State Configuration Revealed* (Apress) and leads Bangalore PowerShell and Bangalore IT Pro user groups. He can be seen speaking regularly at local user group events and conferences in India and abroad about topics ranging from PowerShell to Azure Services.

Acknowledgments

Pranab—There are so many people whom, without their support and encouragement, I could not have written this book. First and foremost, my parents (Maa and Baba). They have always been my pillar of strength. Thank you to my wife (Meenakshi) for being so supportive and helping me write this. She actually pushed me to go for it with my hectic days at work. My lovely little daughter (Preesha), who is my world; she actually let me write when it was probably time to play/spend time with her. Several others supported me unconditionally, including my elder sister (Rupa Chatterjee). Thank you for the faith you have in me; I am here at Microsoft because of you. Thanks also to my brother-in-law (Anindya Chatterjee), for motivating me and inspiring me when I needed him most. I would also like to thank my in-laws for believing that I could do this and supporting me. I would like to express my gratitude to all my mentors, colleagues, and friends at Microsoft, as well as all my managers for being supportive about this idea. A big thank you to the Apress team, including John, who encouraged me to write and Prachi, for being so flexible with the timeline. A special thanks to all the reviewers.

Sourabh—A special note of thanks to my wife Sharie, who was very encouraging and supportive of the long hours I put in during the course of the book. I would like to dedicate this book to my mentors, to my teachers for their invaluable lessons, and finally to the publishers for being accommodating and very supportive of our requests.

Amit—A special note of thanks to my wife for being supportive when I worked on this book after spending hours at the office. Without her, this book would not have been possible. She was the one who actually pushed me to write this book. I would like to dedicate my contribution to the book to my mom and dad, who always believed that nothing is impossible if you put your heart into it. And as always, my gratitude goes out to my mentors who have made it possible for me to learn about this ever-evolving product in a seamless manner. Last but not the least, thanks to Apress for being flexible with the schedule and super accommodating, which really helped us complete this book.

CHAPTER 1

∎ ∎ ∎

Introduction to Microsoft Azure

The cloud has become an important consideration in any meeting that you have with an IT decision maker. The benefits of having a cloud-based system make it attractive to adopt a private, public, or even a hybrid cloud. However, it is interesting to note that the cloud as it's known today existed decades before the word "cloud" became fashionable!

Microsoft provided a large number of cloud services even before the cloud became the *cloud*, for example an e-mail platform like Hotmail. This was and still is a cloud-based personal e-mail service. Another service that Microsoft still hosts is its Xbox Live gaming service, which provides gamers with multiplayer gaming options, profile management, and social gaming experiences.

In this chapter, we will talk about cloud computing and how the concepts relate to Microsoft Azure. We will also look at the different service models and offerings available in Microsoft Azure and discuss some of the common services used with Azure SQL Server deployments.

Cloud Computing Overview

Cloud computing is an innovative platform that is revolutionizing the way we do computing. Cloud computing is based on the key principle of "pay-as-you-go," whereby you don't invest in the hardware or the software for your computing needs, but instead rent the computational power, storage, software, and other resources you need from a vendor. This reduces the overall investment needed. Cloud computing helps users and enterprises get global, highly available, request-based access to compute, storage, and software services. These cloud-based resources (compute, storage, or the software services) are based on the principles of resource sharing in order to provide a consistent and cost-effective solution.

Cloud computing relies heavily on the concept of *virtualization*, where physical computing resources can be divided into multiple independent virtual devices, each of which can be utilized to perform some sort of computing task. Virtualization helps create

Electronic supplementary material The online version of this chapter (doi:10.1007/978-1-4842-2083-2_1) contains supplementary material, which is available to authorized users.

P. Mazumdar et al., *Pro SQL Server on Microsoft Azure*, DOI 10.1007/978-1-4842-2083-2_1

a highly scalable and agile system of computing units, which can be allocated and utilized on demand. Virtualization also helps reduce the hardware infrastructure related costs by better utilizing the existing hardware resources.

One of the most important design principles for any cloud computing environment is to make the best, effective, or optimal use of the shared resources. Since cloud resources are shared by multiple users and have the flexibility of being allocated on demand, effective use of these resources is of paramount importance. The ability to effectively utilize the shared resources reduces the overall cost to run and maintain the cloud computing environment.

Cloud computing provides a shift from the traditional CAPEX (capital expenditure) model, where organizations invest in acquiring fixed assets that depreciate over time, to an OPEX (operational expenditure) model, where the organization invests in operational expenses incurred during usage of services relying on a shared infrastructure. The phrase "migration to cloud" indicates this movement from the CAPEX to the OPEX model. The key points driving this migration to cloud infrastructure are:

- Cloud computing helps businesses reduce initial costs of setting up data centers or other server environments as required so they can instead focus the time and energies on their core business and projects.

- Since cloud computing resources or services can be provisioned and adjusted on demand, it helps reduce the "go-to-market" time for organizations and to meet the fluctuating demands of their business.

Characteristics of Cloud Computing

The key characteristics of any cloud computing environment are:

- *Agility*: Cloud computing platforms are characterized by the agility with which new features and services can be introduced and how a new computing resource or a service could be spun out and become consumable.

- *Cost*: Cloud computing platforms enable an organization to transition from a CAPEX model to an OPEX model. This helps reduce the initial cost for setting up a computing platform or in adopting newer technologies. A majority of the vendors that provide a cloud computing platform offer a pay-as-you-go model, which means consumers only pay for what they use.

- *Device and location independence*: Cloud computing enables users and organizations to access their resources over the Internet, meaning the resources can be accessed from anywhere, regardless of which data center the resources are located in.

- *Maintenance*: Since most of the maintenance is managed by the cloud computing vendor, consumers do not need to invest time and resources in maintenance.

- *Resource sharing*: Since cloud computing is built on the principles of resource sharing, it allows the vendors to:

  a. Centralize their infrastructure in geographical locations with lower costs for real estates, electricity, etc.

  b. Effectively and efficiently use the computing resources.

- *Scalability and elasticity*: Cloud computing allows for dynamic, quick and near real-time provisioning of resources and services. This helps users scale up or down their use in accordance with their business needs.

- *Reliability*: Cloud computing platforms use multiple redundant sites. both local (same data center) and geo redundancy to provide for better business continuity and disaster recovery.

Service Models

As shown in Figure 1-1, most cloud computing providers provide services in the following service models: platform, infrastructure, and software.

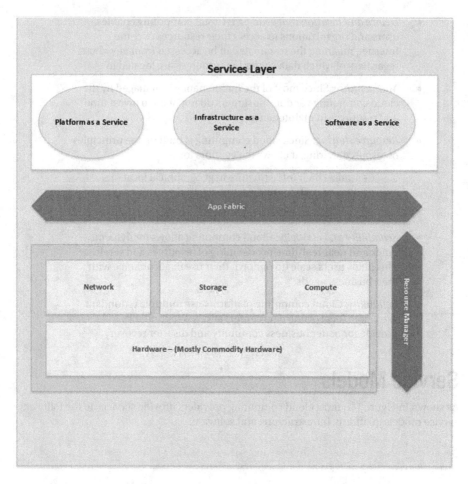

Figure 1-1. Representational view—service models

Platform as a Service

While the SaaS model can be the perfect solution for a majority of the software needs of an organization, the absence of the ability to customize and change the services as per the business needs make it unusable for some organizations. Since there is no customization available, SaaS services sometimes don't fit the needs of every aspect of a user's business. In such cases, businesses have to invest time and resources in building software capabilities to address these gaps. Thankfully, cloud computing provides the Platform as a Service (PaaS) model, which can fill this gap and allow consumers to create and run custom applications. PaaS offers cloud-hosted application servers with very high scalability and elasticity.

In the PaaS model, the cloud vendors provide a pre-configured, virtualized application server environment, to which organization or users can deploy their custom in-house build applications. The cloud vendor ensures the maintenance, patching, and availability of the app servers, and the organizations need to manage and maintain the custom applications running on the app servers. During deployment of these applications, the developers define the resource requirements (CPU, network, memory, and so on) for these applications. The cloud computing provision engine consumes this resource requirement definition (most as part of a configuration file) and creates and binds the necessary infrastructures needed to run the application. PaaS is an ideal solution for new applications being built by the customers, as migrating legacy applications might require extensive application redesign to comply with the rules of the PaaS model.

Infrastructure as a Service

The Infrastructure as a Service (IaaS) model provides hosted server environments, which can be used to deploy and run software services. IaaS is very similar to what organizations have been traditionally doing, where they build physical or virtualized servers on-premises and run their software on these servers. The difference between IaaS and the traditional approach is that, in the IaaS world, the servers are hosted in vendor's data centers, rather than the enterprise's data center. This can be perceived as a rent-a-server model, where the organizations pay for the use of the servers on an as-needed basis. In the IaaS model, users have full control over what software runs on these servers, the DR and high availability requirements, and the customization needed for the software. Depending on the vendor, the users may also have the flexibility to upsize or downsize the servers as per demand. Additionally, depending on the vendor and the type of server provisioned, the server may include additional software, such as the operating system, an Exchange server, or an RDBMS server.

Given the flexibility and ability to customize the provisioned server, IaaS can be used to migrate legacy applications easily to the cloud, but build a cloud server that mimics the on-premises server configurations.

Software as a Service

The Software as a Service (or SaaS) model helps users consume software services hosted by a cloud computing vendor. In the SaaS model, cloud computing vendors host a software service or application and make it accessible to customers in a subscription-based model. The customers use these services on a pay-as-you-go basis. Given that SaaS is based on a subscription-based usage model, the users have a choice to suspend, stop, reduce, or increase their use of the services.

In the SaaS model, the software service configuration and the underlying hardware infrastructure are not accessible to the end users. As such, users cannot change the services or features offered. SaaS offers a highly sharable multi-tenant environment, where thousands and millions of users can operate at the same time, in a mutually exclusive and highly secure context. SaaS also offers a very agile platform, which can help users reduce their "go-to-market" time and help them focus on their core business projects without worrying about the IT challenges of managing and maintaining an environment for their IT needs.

Microsoft Azure

Azure is a cloud computing platform developed by Microsoft for creating, deploying, and managing applications and services through a global network of Microsoft managed or Microsoft partner hosted data centers. Azure provides cloud-based services in all the three service models: Software as a Service (SaaS), Platform as a Service (PaaS), and Infrastructure as a Service (IaaS).

Azure provides a cloud-hosted server and the other infrastructure resources like storage, network, and other integration infrastructure for creating, deploying, and running applications. Azure relies on massive groups of commodity, off-the-shelf hardware in providing the cloud computing environment. Figure 1-2 shows a representational Azure resource model where application servers along with storage, network, and other compute resources are provisioned on demand by the policies set during deployment. The Azure Fabric Controller, with its dedicated set of highly redundant and highly available servers and software, is the intelligence behind the entire Azure environment.

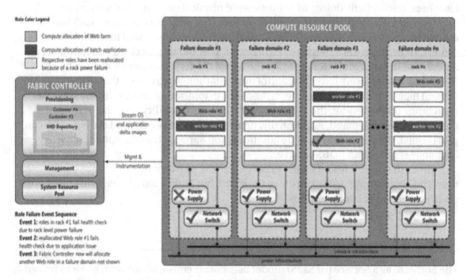

Figure 1-2. Representational resource model—Microsoft Azure

Azure compute resource pool consists of a very large pool of commodity hardware resources, which are configured in a highly redundant and highly available setup. This high availability and redundancy is maintained and managed by the Azure Fabric Controller.

The Fabric Controller is designed to detect any kind of failures and take necessary action to mitigate the risks of those failures. These actions could include spawning new resources and migrating the resources to a different pool of hardware resources. The Fabric Controller is also responsible for upsizing or downsizing the resources based on user requests.

Azure Services

Azure offers a plethora of services, which are grouped together in different categories, as illustrated in Figure 1-3. Some of the services that are used commonly or are needed with SQL deployments in Azure are discussed below.

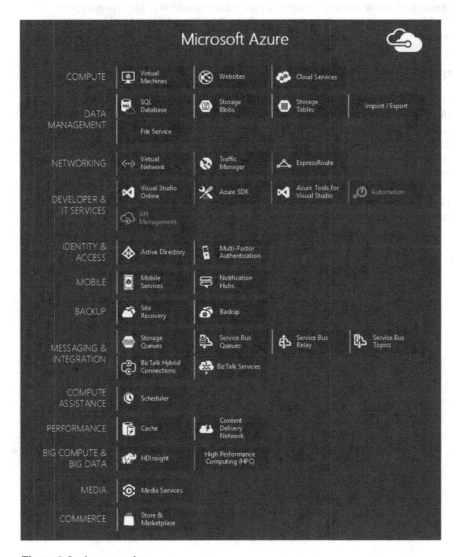

Figure 1-3. *Azure services*

Compute Offerings

Microsoft Azure provides three important compute offerings, which can be utilized to run web sites and applications. The Azure web sites and Azure Cloud Services use Azure Virtual Machines to run the web sites and applications, while abstracting the tasks of managing the creation and administrations from the users. These two services provide PaaS offerings, while the third option—Azure Virtual Machine (VMs)—provides full control to the users, to create and manage their VMs. Azure Virtual Machines provides an IaaS offering.

Virtual Machines

Azure Virtual Machines provides users with complete control over the creation, configuration, and management of the virtual machines and the applications running on them. Azure Virtual Machines allows for creating of VMs using VHDs uploaded to Azure or by leveraging VHD images available in the Azure VHD gallery, as illustrated in Figure 1-4. Azure provides a plethora of VHDs for different editions/versions of Windows, Linux, and other server applications, such as SQL Server, BiTalk, Oracle, etc.

Azure Virtual Machines allows configuration and addition of multiple virtual disks to a VM. These disks can be configured either on the Standard Storage or the Solid State Devices (SSDs) based Premium Storage.

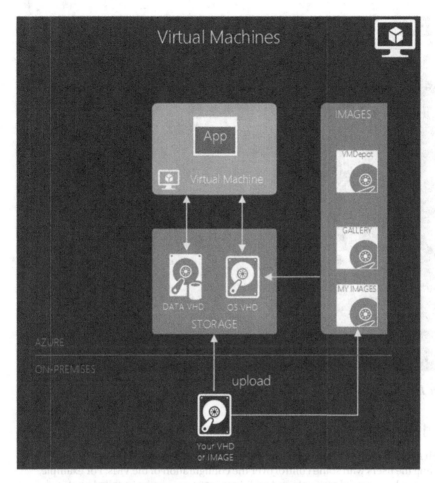

Figure 1-4. *Azure Virtual Machines*

Azure WebApps (Formerly Azure Websites)

Azure WebApps, formerly Azure Websites, provides a managed web environment using the Azure Management portal as well as APIs. Apart from the ability to create new web sites on the cloud, Azure WebApps also allows for the migration of any existing web sites to the cloud. WebApps provides the ability to upsize or downsize the resources on demand. Creating an Azure WebApps service basically creates a VM with IIS and associated storage, as illustrated in Figure 1-5. The creation and management of these VMs is encapsulated from the end users.

Azure WebApps is available in both a Share Tenant model, where resources are shared between multiple web sites, and a Standard model, which provides dedicated resources to the web site. The ability to upsize or downsize the instances is only available with Standard model.

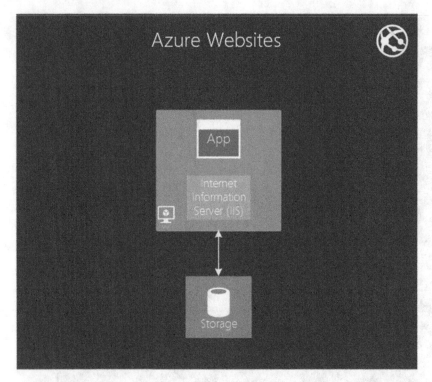

Figure 1-5. *Azure WebApps*

Cloud Services

As with Azure Websites, Azure cloud services use VMs to execute workloads, while providing the users with some control over the configuration of the VMs. For example, the VMs can be accessed remotely and additional software can be installed on the VMs. Azure Cloud services provide two different variants of VMs. Instances of web roles run a variant of Windows Server with IIS, while instances of worker roles run the same Windows Server variant without IIS. A cloud services application relies on some combination of these two options.

Data Management Offerings

Windows Azure provides several ways to store and manage data. This diversity of services allows users to utilize Azure to address a variety of business requirements and problems. Azure provides the following four major data management offerings.

SQL/Oracle Running on Azure VM

Azure VMs allow the users to configure an instance of Microsoft SQL Server, Oracle, or any other Database Management System. As earlier mentioned in the section on compute offerings and Virtual Machines, multiple images are available in the Azure marketplace, and they can be used deploy a SQL Server instance (SQL 2012, SQL 2014 and SQL 2016 RC releases, as of writing this book) or an Oracle instance. Moreover, other DBMS environments can be created using a customized VHD, which can be uploaded to Azure.

Azure SQL Database

The Azure SQL Database is a relational database as a service, which provides all the important features of an RDBMS, including transaction consistency, data integrity, and multi-user concurrent data access system. Azure SQL Database is built on the same principles as the Microsoft SQL Server and provides comparable features. For users who are already familiar with SQL Server, adapting to Azure SQL Database won't be difficult. Azure SQL Database employs a PaaS Service model, where the consumer controls the access patterns, while the platform takes care of other administrative work. Azure SQL Database provides automatic backups and point-in-time restore for the databases. Depending on the service tier being used, Azure SQL Databases also provide high availability options at a reasonable cost.

Azure Blobs

Azure Blobs ("blob storage" and "storage blobs" are the same thing) is a cloud-based inexpensive storage solution for storing unstructured binary data (Figure 1-6). Consider Azure Blob storage as a file store for binary files, with a maximum file size limit of 1TB. Applications can also make use of Azure drives, which let blobs provide persistent storage for a Windows filesystem mounted in an Azure instance. The application sees ordinary Windows files, but the contents are actually stored in a blob.

Blob storage is used by many other Azure features (including Virtual Machines), so it can certainly handle your workloads.

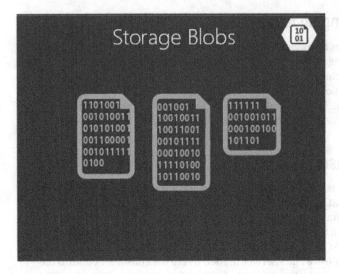

Figure 1-6. *Azure storage blobs*

Azure Table Storage

Tables provide a NoSQL/key-value storage. Tables provide fast, reliable, and simple access to large amounts of loosely structured and unstructured data. Tables provide non-relational or NoSQL storage.

Networking

Azure provides several options to set up private networks, virtual private networks, and network load balancing. The most commonly used options are described next.

Virtual Network

Azure Virtual Network (VNet) is a logical partitioning of the Azure cloud dedicated to the subscription. Administrators have full control over the IPs, the DNS settings, and the security policies for the network. It can be compared to a private network of an organization, which runs behind a firewall. Azure VNets allow you to create subnets, which can be used to further segment the network, depending on requirements. Azure allows users to connect the VNet to their on-premises networks using one of the many connectivity options available with Azure, as illustrated in Figure 1-7.

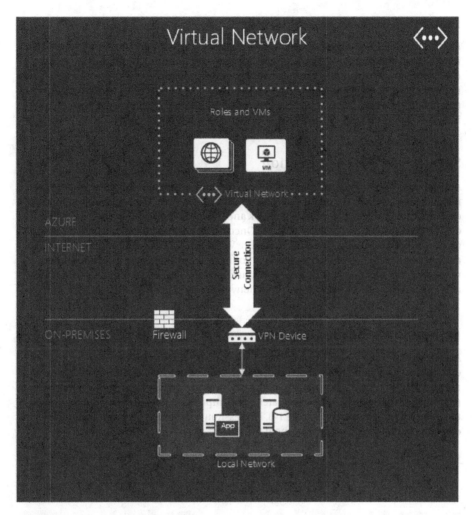

Figure 1-7. *Azure Virtual Network*

VPN Connection Options

Connectivity options allow users to connect their on-premises networks with their Azure networks. These options include:

- Point-to-site VPN connections
- Site-to-site VPN connections
- ExpressRoute connections

Point-to-Site VPN Connection

A point-to-site VPN lets users create a secure connection to their Azure Virtual Networks from a client computer in their on-premises networks. Point-to-site connections have to be configured individually on each client computer that needs to connect to the virtual network. Point-to-site connections do not require a VPN device, but use a VPN client that needs to be installed on each client computer. The VPN is established by manually initiating the connection from the on-premises client computer.

Site-to-Site VPN Connection

A site-to-site VPN allows users to create a secure connection between their on-premises network and and their Azure Virtual Network. Site-to-site VPN connections require a VPN device located on the on-premises network and must be configured to create a secure connection with the Azure VPN Gateway. Once the connection is established, resources on the on-premises network and in the Azure Virtual Network can communicate directly and securely. Unlike the point-to-site VPN connection, site-to-site connections do not require the establishment of a separate connection for each client computer on the local network to access resources in the virtual network.

ExpressRoute Connection

Azure ExpressRoute allows the users to create a private connection between Azure data centers and their on-premises networks. ExpressRoute connections do not go over the public Internet, but instead use a dedicated Internet channel and thus offer more reliability, better security, and lower latencies compared to the typical connections over the Internet. As illustrated in Figure 1-8, ExpressRoute does not use the public Internet to connect your on-premises environment with Azure.

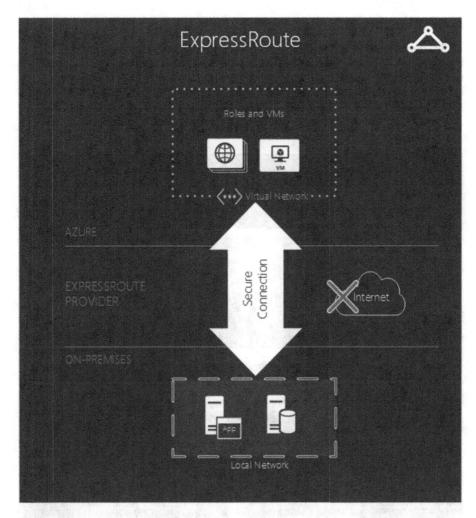

Figure 1-8. *Azure ExpressRoute*

Developer Services

Azure provides several services that can be leveraged by developers to write optimal and performant code. In addition to providing several features to write code, Azure also provides methods to automate testing and capture telemetry while running their applications.

Visual Studio Team Services

Visual Studio Team Services provides a service to develop and ship applications, share codes with the team, track application development, and load-test applications, written in any language

Application Insights

Application Insights is an extensible analytics service that allows users to monitor live performance of their applications. It can help detect and diagnose performance issues and provide telemetry data for applications. Developers can use the service to continuously improve the performance and usability of their application code. Application Insights works with web-based and standalone applications developed using .Net, J2EE, and hosted on on-premises or on the cloud, as illustrated in Figure 1-9.

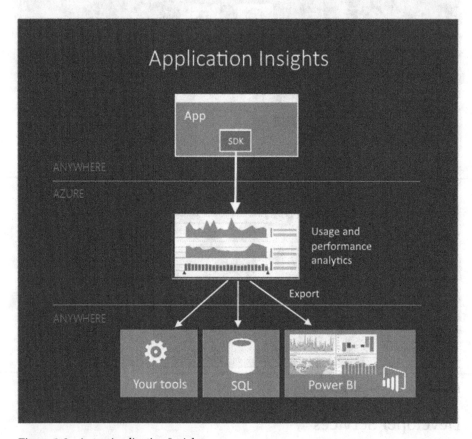

Figure 1-9. *Azure Application Insights*

Identity and Access

Windows Azure Active Directory provides robust and secure identity services that help control and manage directory and access management in the cloud. It also provides a seamless sign-in experience to Azure resources and enhanced security with multi-factor authentication.

Active Directory

Azure Active Directory (AAD) is an identity and access management solution that provides organizations with the ability to manage users and groups, just like an on-premises active directory solution. AAD helps provide secure access to resources on-premises and on the cloud. AAD is available in three service tiers: Free, Basic, and Premium.

Backup

Azure provides a plethora of simple and reliable backup services that can be utilized to ensure business continuity and disaster recovery whenever needed.

Azure Site Recovery

Site Recovery is an Azure service that contributes to your business continuity and disaster recovery (BCDR) strategy by orchestrating replication of your on-premises servers and virtual machines to a secondary on-premises data center, or to Azure. Site Recovery handles the replication, and you can kick off failover and recovery with a simple click.

Summary

In this chapter, we learned the basic principles of cloud computing and the different service models available with cloud computing. We then discussed the Microsoft Cloud Computing platform, which included Azure and some of the key services available with Azure.

CHAPTER 2

■ ■ ■

Azure Architecture

Today cloud computing has matured and has clear demarcations between the different classes of service—platform, software, and infrastructure. Microsoft offers services in all three categories. But before we jump into them, let us first understand the nuances involved in cloud services. In this chapter, we will understand how Infrastructure as a Service (IaaS) works. Think of IaaS as a pizza where your favorite pizza vendor provides the frozen pizza and you need to manage the stuff that is used to warm and serve the pizza. In the IaaS world, this usually means that the vendor provides all the hardware, including the computing power, network, and storage along with its associated services. All you do is use the combination of the infrastructure offerings, which allows you to deploy any application or service on that platform.

Microsoft's Azure platform is not just about hyper-scale abstraction of virtualization fundamentals. There is also a large amount of innovation that Azure drives in the form of its data centers. Let's quickly look at how the hardware behind the concepts described here are laid out. The Microsoft cloud server specification essentially provides the blueprints for the data center servers Microsoft uses to deliver a diverse portfolio of cloud services. They offer dramatic improvements over traditional enterprise server designs: up to 40 percent server cost savings, 15 percent power efficiency gains, and 50 percent reduction in deployment and service times. Microsoft hosts its cloud services on owned and leased data centers across the world, which spans over a million servers and over hundred data centers.

There are some interesting strategic decisions that were made to get Azure to where it is today. The most interesting is the cost factor. Cost is always a discussion point in the IT world and Microsoft decided to reduce cost of hosting these environments by allocating against key cost drivers. This is fundamentally different from how the standard cost calculation works, which involves association of cost with the amount of space used. In contrast, Azure uses key factors like energy consumption, bandwidth consumption, incident response, and server capacity for determining cost.

In 2014, Microsoft contributed the Open Cloud Server design to the Open Compute Project, which allows the industry to benefit from the company's experience in setting up data centers for the various cloud-based services that it managed.

In the next few sections, we will learn how compute, network, and storage is organized in Azure and the internals that you would need to know to make an IaaS offering work for you.

© Pranab Mazumdar, Sourabh Agarwal, Amit Banerjee 2016
P. Mazumdar et al., *Pro SQL Server on Microsoft Azure*, DOI 10.1007/978-1-4842-2083-2_2

The Azure Services

Azure today offers a multitude of services in all three categories—PaaS, SaaS, and IaaS—and it keeps growing. The biggest challenge about writing a book on Azure is not whether the book will remain current after you have written it but whether it remains current while you are writing it. The world of sprints, shortened release cycles, and agile development methods ensures that the consumer of technology receives the technology content as quickly as possible.

Instead of naming the various services that Azure offers today, you will just learn about the different areas that Azure can help you and your business. In the recent times, Azure has increasingly sought to gain parity between what you are used to in the on-premises world and what you see in action in Azure. This means that the lines between your data centers and the Azure data centers are becoming increasingly fuzzy and a user of your platform will very rarely be able to gauge the difference between what is running on Azure and on-premise (unless you put a banner on their application that proclaimed its host data center).

Azure today offers services for:

- Management and security like key value and operational insights

- Developer services like Visual Studio Team Services

- Identity and access management like Azure Active Directory, multifactor authentication

- Hybrid integration like BizTalk, Site recovery

- Media and CDN like media encoding, media indexer

- Internet of Things (IoT), like Event Hub, Stream Analytics

- Analytics like Data Lake, HDInsight, Machine Learning, Data Factory

- Data and Storage like SQL Database, DocumentDB, SQL Data Warehouse

- Web and mobile like Web Apps, API Management

As you see, Azure is more than just a bunch of hardware running your virtual machines. All of these solutions make use of certain parts of Azure's compute, storage, and networking. In the next few chapters, we will delve deep into the internals of the Azure's compute, storage, and networking, but in this chapter, we will understand how all of this is tied together.

The Compute

The compute in Azure is a combination of processing power and physical memory. When you start deploying compute in Azure, you are essentially spawning a virtual machine with an operating system backed by local storage that hosts the operating system files and a temporary storage. The local storage solution is not recommended for hosting your application or any data that your application might need. There might be situations where you use your ephemeral storage, which is referred to as the D drive. Examples are explained in later chapters.

Azure offers different tiers of compute that attract different sets of pricing (see Figure 2-1). The pricing is similar to your cellular minutes. You pay for every minute of usage. So if your virtual machine is up and running, you are paying for the compute power. Whether you are using the compute power or not is immaterial. Again similar to your cellular minutes. Your usage gets accounted for whether you talk or stay silent on the call. It is very important to understand what kind of physical memory and processing power you require to host your application or service.

The next question on your mind would be what can you host. Well it's an empty house! You can literally host anything you want as you would on a virtual machine hosted in on-premise data center. The inherent advantage of using cloud-based infrastructure services is you have to click a button and the magic happens in the background. Spawning up the virtual machine, setting up the operating system, and tying the compute, network, and storage together is done by Azure infrastructure. Your job is to just provide the inputs!

Another advantage of hosting in the cloud is the packaged deployment offering, namely the gallery image. You can spawn up a virtual machine with software solutions preconfigured. Azure Virtual Machines support SQL Server, Oracle, IBM, SAP, and much more. The endearing aspect of such a one-click deployment is the license cost can be baked into it if you pick a solution-based image like SQL Server, Oracle, etc. If you don't want to have the license cost baked into your per-minute cost for compute, then you can use your own license and use Azure's automation offering to run your post virtual machine deployment steps.

Let's now quickly understand about compute tiers that are available in Azure. For example, the Basic tier (A0, A1, A2 ... An) consists of machines as small as 1 core and 0.75GB of RAM with 20GB local disk attached to it. You would pay approximately $13 if you left a virtual machine with this configuration running for an entire month. On the other end of the spectrum, you currently have the G-series machines which provide 32 virtual CPUs and 448GB of physical memory.

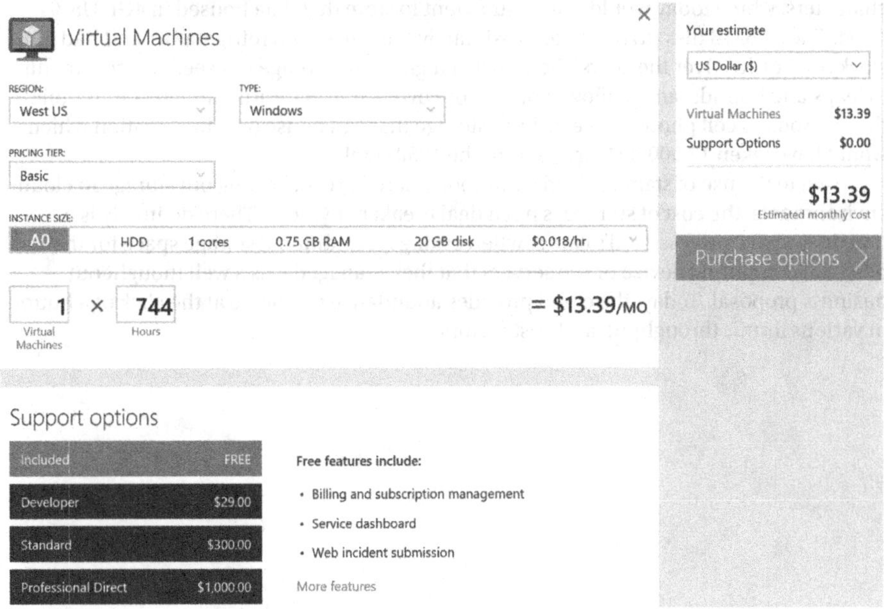

Figure 2-1. Azure pricing calculator

As you can see, there is a wide range that allows you to pick the right combination for your business.

The compute provides elasticity, which is what the cloud is famous for, by allowing you to scale out as per your load requirements. A scale out capability is not required when you are deploying SQL Server as a standalone SQL Server does not have scale out capabilities. There are features in SQL Server that allow you to scale out with the help of replication or availability groups. You can scale up and scale down your virtual machine instances as and when you need or even to your whims and fancies. While a whim and fancy might not be sufficient business reason, you can definitely use the trends from your compute baselines to scale up and scale down! Elasticity is becoming ubiquitous in the compute world today and public cloud makes that a reality. One of the most common scenarios for retailers is to match the holiday season traffic burst. This typically leads to over-provisioning of hardware throughout the year for a peak season that lasts less than a month at times. Elasticity in the cloud makes this a reality! Azure provides an auto-scaling feature that allows you to scale your workload running on web roles, worker roles, or virtual machines. Virtual machines are turned on or turned off from an availability set of previously created machines when you scale an application running on Azure IaaS. One of the options is to specify scaling based on the average percentage of CPU usage.

Some of the common conundrums in a hosted or on-premise data center are not really issues in Azure.

The Storage

In the previous section, you understood how Azure compute ties what we know as physical memory and processing power as a cohesive unit. This section explains what it means to store data in Azure. In the 1950s, the first hard drive stored five million six-bit characters, which today would not be sufficient to store that data housed in 4GB USB drive. The 3.75MB disk drive was approximately the size of two refrigerators and had a stack of 50 disks! Over the years, the world of digital data storage has seen improvements in leaps and bounds, and it allows you to store over 64GB of information in your mobile device. Today's cell phones have in-built storage that can house over information which would have taken 17,000 disk drives from the 1950s era!

Due to the use of standardized commodity hardware for scaling out storage in cloud environments, the cost of storage is not a deal breaker anymore! There definitely is a time in every IT professional's career when asking for additional storage space for their personal computing device or the servers that they managed was a well thought out business proposal. Today, the cloud provides abundance of storage at the click of a button in various forms, throughput, and cost factors.

Azure storage provides the storage foundation for all Azure Virtual Machines. It encompasses all the tenets of cloud, which means Azure storage is scalable, durable, and highly available. Once again, the advantage of cloud is that you pay for what you use and when you use it. It's a like a pay-as-you-go cell phone subscription.

Azure Storage uses an auto-partitioning system that automatically load-balances your data based on traffic. As the demands for storage of your application grow, Azure Storage automatically allocates the appropriate storage resources to meet them.

Like any Azure component, Azure Storage is accessible from anywhere in the world. One unique aspect of Azure Storage is that any type of application, whether it's running in the cloud or desktop or on-premises or mobile or tablet device, can access Azure Storage services. Advanced concepts and design decisions for Azure storage will be explained in detail in Chapter 3 of this book.

Now it is time to understand briefly how the storage in Microsoft's Azure platform is organized. As shown in Figure 2-2, storage is organized in different formats—blobs, tables, queues, and files. Storage is organized in the form of containers, tables, queues, and shares. Think of each of these as the storage containers in your kitchen. You typically had different container with different attributes storing our cereals, flour, rice, etc. Similarly, the storage in Azure is segregated into containers of a particular type.

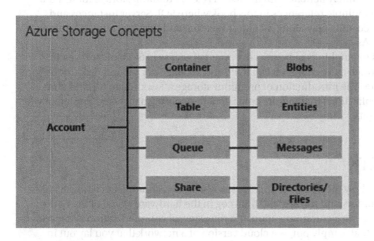

Figure 2-2. Azure storage concepts

Blob storage is essentially a binary representation of any storage object that you place in an Azure blob container. Each blob store can host documents, media files, executables, and basically any object that you want to store in the cloud. These are typically used to host raw data and media-related files like music, pictures, videos, etc.

Table storage can be used to house structured datasets, which is a NoSQL key-attribute data store used for fast programmatic access to large quantities of data.

Queue storage provides reliable messaging for workflow processing and for communication between components of cloud services. The messages could flow between any application endpoints. This could either applications hosted on the cloud or in our data center.

File storage offers SMB-based file shares but the difference is that these are hosted on the cloud. These shared have a cloud-based path that any application can access as long as it is connected to the Internet.

Since the cloud hosts applications of various types, the throughput and performance requirements vary for each and every business. This is something that Azure storage provides in the form of Standard and Premium storage.

The main design goal of Azure Premium storage was to provide high performance, low latency disks for virtual machines that run I/O intensive workloads. Certain SQL Server workloads definitely benefit from the use of Azure Premium storage for its data disks. You will find multiple references in this book where SQL Server instances and premium storage accounts play along nicely for meeting and beating your performance and throughput SLAs.

If you wanted to put things in perspective, you get access to 64TB of storage per virtual machine, which can achieve 80,000 IOPS and 2000MB per second disk throughput per virtual machine. The introduction of premium storage allows you to lift-and-shift your enterprise applications that require consistent high performance and low latency for their IO requirements.

The Network

Before we dive into how the compute and the storage layer communicate with each other, it is important to understand the last and final cog in the hardware wheel of the Azure platform. The interservice communication and the external communication is handled by a network layer that, simply put, is a cloud version of a network that you lay out in an enterprise environment. Figure 2-3 illustrates a typical network configuration in an enterprise.

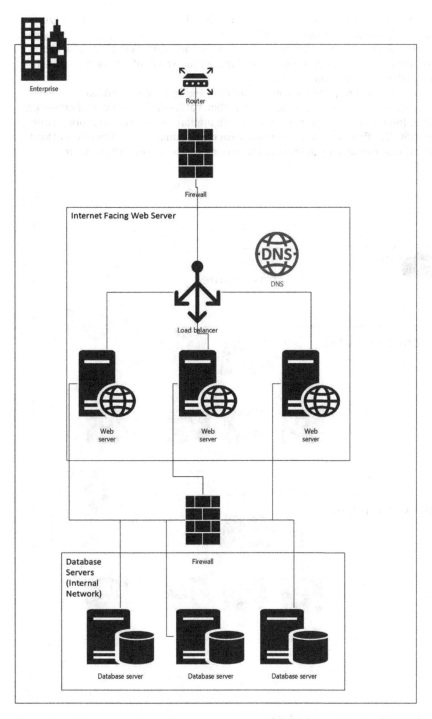

Figure 2-3. *Network configuration of an on-premises environment*

25

Azure Virtual Network is a representation of the all things networking in the Azure data centers. It compartmentalizes your IP address blocks, DNS settings, security policies, and route tables associated with your Azure subscription. Azure networking also allows you to stretch your on-premises network and make your Azure subscription objects are an extended part of the actual network.

If you want to draw parallels, you will notice in Figure 2-4 that the Azure infrastructure takes on the role of the router. It allows access from your virtual network to the public Internet without the need of any configuration. Think of the network security groups (NSGs) as firewalls that are applied to each individual subnet. The physical load balancers are substituted by Internet facing and internal load balancers in Azure.

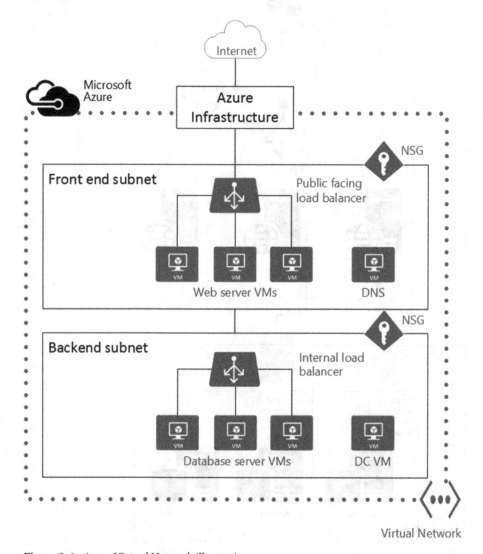

Figure 2-4. *Azure Virtual Network illustration*

A very pertinent question at this point would be to question the need for a virtual network. The reasons are many. Apart from providing the *connectivity layer* for connecting between various Azure services and virtual machines, there is a need for *isolation* which allows you to create disjoint networks for various functions like development, testing, and production that use the same CIDR address blocks. Azure also provides *internal name resolution* for your virtual machines and PaaS role instances deployed in your virtual network (VNet). You can also deploy your own DNS servers and configure the VNet to use them.

One of the interesting challenges of the modern day network administrator is to provide network connectivity to the outer world, a.k.a. the Internet, without compromising security. Azure networking makes public Internet connectivity possible without compromising on security with the help of network security groups (NSGs).

Let's quickly understand what network security groups are and their role in the Azure networking architecture. If you had to draw an analogy, then the network security group (NSG) is basically a watchdog for the network traffic that originates between your Azure subscription objects and the internal as well as external client(s) that connect to these objects. You can create NSGs to control the inbound and outbound traffic to the networking components like network interfaces (NICs), virtual machines, and subnets. You can use NSGs to decide whether or not network traffic is approved or denied based on source IP address and port or destination IP address or port. The NSG behavior is similar to firewalls in an enterprise environment.

Azure networking is covered in detail in Chapter 4.

How It Works Together

Now that you understand the basics of the building blocks available in Azure, it is important to understand how it all works together. If you had to look at an Infrastructure as a Service option in Azure, Figure 2-5 would show you how a virtual machine in Azure is laid out.

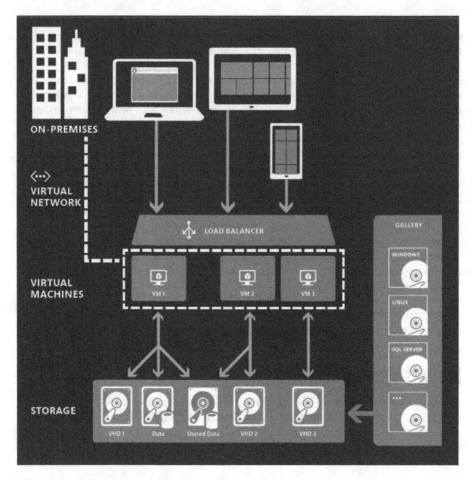

Figure 2-5. *An Azure Virtual Machine*

Figure 2-5 shows that Azure networking is the communication gateway between the external clients and the Azure Virtual Machines. One of the most interesting facts to note is that the storage layer is a completely separate physical entity. This is fundamentally different from how servers are structured in the data center. If someone wanted to draw a parallel, the storage layer could be envisioned as a marriage between a storage area network (SAN) and network attached storage (NAS). The disk arrays are managed in a scalable and elastic manner by the storage layer, which communicates with the compute layer over a very fast network.

You can choose to deploy an Azure gallery image, which is a pre-cooked image available from Microsoft and other third parties, to host the operating system and pre-installed software of your choice. This way, you don't have to write a single installer!

Infrastructure as a Service is just one of the service models that makes use of the compute, storage, and networking. In the on-premises world, a common deployment model is a web application, which consists of a three-tier architecture. The first tier is the client application, which is typically a web browser that connects to the middle tier, which is the application server. The application server connects to the backend server, which is typically a data store. A similar architecture can be achieved in Azure using web roles as the frontend, worker roles as the middle tier, and the data store (SQL server, blobs, NoSQL, etc.) as the third tier. Figure 2-6 illustrates a typical three-tier application architecture hosted on Azure.

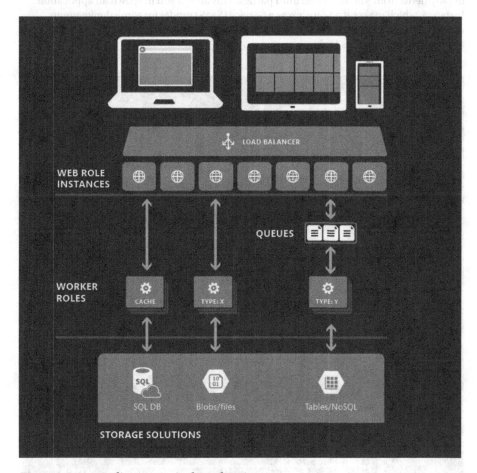

Figure 2-6. *An application service hosted on Azure*

In Figure 2-6, the clients connect using Azure Virtual Network to a web role instance, which is a compute resource running the web application. Depending on the application's need, the number of instances can be configured to scale up or down, which makes the service elastic out-of-the-box without having the developer to do anything specific. The storage comes into play depending on whether the application uses the Azure Storage entities for storing data like blobs or queues. An indirect use of the storage would be if a relational or non-relational Platform as a Service (PaaS) offering is used that internally makes use of the storage offering. Figure 2-6 shows the Azure SQL database as a storage option. This will be covered in detail later in this book.

Another deployment paradigm in Azure is to host application instances. These are not just limited to web applications but can be used on any kind of applications like mobile, services, APIs, etc. The Azure marketplace offers a plethora of pre-built service deployments from Microsoft and third parties. This allows you to spawn an application instance, which makes it a Software as a Service (SaaS) model for some deployments and Platform as a Service (PaaS) model for other deployments. Figure 2-7 shows how application deployments look.

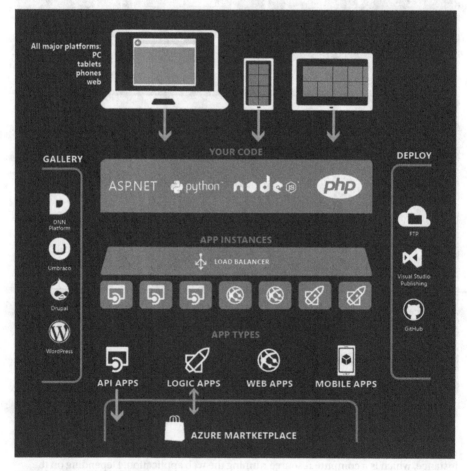

Figure 2-7. *Azure App instances*

As you can see from the previous figures, Azure abstracts the deployment mechanics, decouples the hardware, and ties the various components together during deployment.

Update/Upgrade Domain

Now that you understand how the architecture is organized for the resource providers, it is imperative to understand the concept of update domains. Think of the *update domain* as a group of servers that you would patch in a maintenance schedule. If you are not the business owner, you need to ensure that the updates have little to no downtime for the applications hosted on the servers that are being patched. This is truly one of the most difficult IT problems in the real world.

Azure distributes instances evenly into multiple upgrade domains, with each upgrade domain acting as one logical unit of a deployment. When upgrading a deployment, the upgrade is carried out one upgrade domain at a time to minimize downtime for the services or applications running on these environments. Upgrade domains help reduce the impact of an upgrade to a running service and at the same time keep the environment up-to-date. This minimizes the risk of known issues affecting production environments due to lack of updates.

It is important to grasp this concept, as having an update domain alone will not help your SQL Server deployment. Even in a failover cluster or availability group environment, SQL Server instances can have only one active node where the service is running. So if the server running your SQL Server instance is rebooted, your database service will go down. It is important to have an Availability Group deployment for any production SQL Server environment hosted on Azure Virtual Machines to prevent extended downtimes.

Fault Domain

As noted earlier, the upgrade/update domain alone is not sufficient for maintaining the uptime of a SQL Server instance hosted on an Azure Virtual Machine. The scope of a single point of failure in Azure is essentially a fault domain.

The easiest way to draw a parallel with the on-premises world is to think of a failover cluster that prevents a single point of failure from a compute standpoint. Now extending this to the world of Azure, a single compute source connected to a power outlet is a fault domain. This could even be a rack in a data center since a power outage in a rack will take out multiple compute nodes from the infrastructure. The fault domain is determined by Azure during deployment and it is highly recommended to have two or more instances of each role deployed in Azure so that a single failure in a fault domain does not result in a service outage for your application. From a SQL Server hosted on an Azure Virtual Machine, it is always recommended to have a primary and secondary deployment from a high availability standpoint. This concept is followed in most enterprise environments and the need to do so in Azure remains. The SLAs are mentioned in the Azure service level agreements.

Deployment

One of the most common tasks when working with Azure is deployment. This used to be a one-way street until recently. Azure now has two deployment models: classic and resource manager. It is best to use the resource manager deployment model for any new development work as much as possible. All Azure resources support one or both deployment models.

There are some important considerations when working with virtual machines using these two deployment models:

- Virtual machines deployed with the classic deployment model cannot be included in a virtual network deployed with Resource Manager.

- Virtual machines deployed with the Resource Manager deployment model must be included in a virtual network.

- Virtual machines deployed with the classic deployment model don't have to be included in a virtual network.

Classic Deployment Model

Azure initially introduced a deployment model called the *classic* deployment model. For this section, we will be restricting the discussion of the deployment of virtual machines. In the classic way of doing things, a deployed virtual machine would be accessible only through a cloud service. The cloud service is a container for holding the virtual machines. The cloud service name had the format *<name>.cloudapp.net*.

Resource Manager Deployment Model

In the Resource Manager deployment model, cloud service is no longer an object required for creating a virtual machine (see Figure 2-8). The Azure Resource Manager enables you to easily leverage pre-built application templates or construct an application template to deploy and manage compute, network, and storage resources on Azure. The templates are available in the increasingly popular JSON format and are easily exported from an existing deployment and applied to a new deployment.

Azure resource providers support the individual resources for creating functioning virtual machines in the configuration that you need. For virtual machines, there are three main resource providers:

- *Compute Resource Provider (CRP)*: Supports instances of virtual machines and optional availability sets.

- *Storage Resource Provider (SRP)*: Supports required storage accounts that store the VHDs for virtual machines, including their operating system and additional data disks.

- *Network Resource Provider (NRP)*: Supports required NICs, virtual machine IP addresses, and subnets within virtual networks and optional load balancers, load balancer IP addresses, and Network Security Groups.

We did discuss the fact that none of these resource providers can work in isolation, as hosting a simple virtual machine requires relationships between the resources in the resource providers. An example of this is that a virtual machine depends on a specific storage account defined in the SRP to store its disks in blob storage. A virtual machine references a specific NIC defined in the NRP and may also have an availability set defined in the CRP. A NIC references the virtual machine's assigned IP address, the subnet of the virtual network for the virtual machine, and to a Network Security Group if gated access is required.

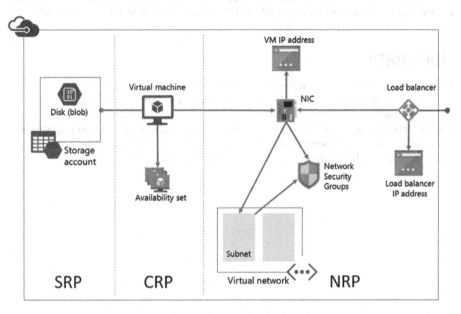

Figure 2-8. *Azure resource providers and their relationships for an Azure Virtual Machine*

Resource Manager (ARM) makes is really simple to build, integrate, and collaborate on complicated applications that can include the entire gamut of Azure resources (such as web sites, SQL databases, virtual machines, and virtual networks) from a shareable template file. Such a shared template file can be used as repeatable deployments for setting up development environments with relative ease.

There is a deep integration of VM extensions (Custom Scripts, DSC, Chef, Puppet, etc.) with the Azure Resource Manager in a template file, which allows easy orchestration of in-VM setup configuration. ARM also allows simple and precise organizational resource access management using Azure Role-Based Access Control (RBAC).

Deployment Automation

Now that we are talking about deployment, an obvious question is if there is a way to automate the actual deployment. Azure provides three different ways to manipulate the compute, storage, and networking objects. The first being the web user interface, which is expected as this is the company that made graphical user interface a commodity. The second and third methods are mainly for programmatically deploying whatever can be deployed using the web portal.

Azure exposes PowerShell cmdlets and REST APIs, which allow developers and IT administrators to write deployment routines. These routines automate the creation of the Azure entity and configure the post deployment configuration options exposed by the entity. The automation capabilities of Azure Automation service, when combined with these programmatic interfaces, are immensely powerful and allow customized workflows to be designed for deployment. A number of such examples can be found on GitHub.

Summary

In this chapter, you learned how Azure defines its compute, storage, and networking boundaries. While there is a layer of abstraction provided in Azure to make your deployment and daily operations easier, the parallels that you can draw with your on-premises environment are similar. This allows for a lower learning curve when migrating to Azure. Infrastructure as a Service has the highest similarity coefficient between your data center and Azure. The similarity wanes as you move from IaaS to PaaS to SaaS.

CHAPTER 3

■ ■ ■

Microsoft Azure Storage

Microsoft Azure Storage is a cloud storage system that provides customers the flexibility to store huge amount of data, and it can be stored for any duration. This uniqueness of the data that is stored here is that you can access the data anywhere and at anytime. It's also a utility-based storage system (i.e., you pay for what you use and what you store). In Microsoft Azure Storage, the data is durable due to the local replication and geographic replication that enables disaster recovery. The storage consists of blobs (user's files), tables (structured storage), and queues (messaging). The data is highly durable, available, and massively scalable. It is exposed through REST APIs, client libraries in .NET, Java, Node.js, Python, PHP, Ruby.

Azure Storage Service

There are several types of Microsoft Azure Storage services (see Figure 3-1):

- Blob storage service
- Table storage
- Queue storage
- File storage

© Pranab Mazumdar, Sourabh Agarwal, Amit Banerjee 2016
P. Mazumdar et al., *Pro SQL Server on Microsoft Azure*, DOI 10.1007/978-1-4842-2083-2_3

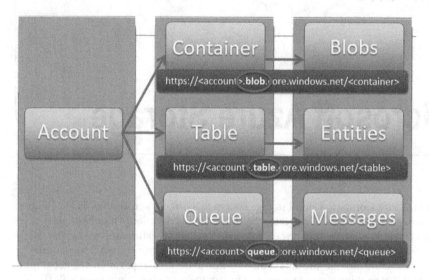

Figure 3-1. *Microsoft Azure Data Storage concepts and REST protocols to access blobs tables and queues*

Blob Storage

A blobs is nothing but a filesystem in the cloud. It can contain text data or binary data, such as a document, a media file, or an application installer. In short, it is a simple interface to store and retrieve files in the cloud (see Figure 3-1). The following list provides some common uses of blobs:

- *Data sharing.* Customers can share documents, pictures, videos, and music.

- *Big Data insights.* Customers can store lots of raw data in the cloud and can compute using map reduce jobs for getting data insights.

- *Backups.* Many customers store the backups in the cloud, i.e., they store on-premises data in the cloud.

The blob storage service contains the following key concepts:

- *Storage accounts.* Microsoft Azure provides storage in the different locations around the world. You need to create a storage account to access the storage services and host your data. Once you create your storage account, you can create blobs and store them in the container, and you can create tables and put entities into those tables. You can also create queues and store messages in those queues.

- *Containers*. A container provides a grouping of all blobs. A storage account could contain more than one container and each container can contain multiple blobs.

- *Blob*. A blob can contain text data or binary data, such as a document, a media file, or an application installer. Microsoft Azure Storage offers three types of blobs:

    - *Block blob*. As it goes, a block blob comprises of blocks, each of which is identified by a block ID. Basically, you create/modify a block blob by writing a set of blocks and committing them by their block IDs. Each block can be of different size with maximum of 4MB. The maximum size of the block blob is 200GB, with a single block containing 50,000 blocks. For writing a block blob no more than 64MB in size, you can upload it in a single write operation. If a block exceeds the size specified within the storage clients, it is broken into smaller chunks.

    - *Page blob*. This is a collection of 512 bytes page optimized for random read and write operations. You need to initialize the page blob and set the maximum size the page blob will grow. For adding/modifying the contents within a page blob, you have to specify an offset and the range that aligns to the 512-byte page boundary. The writes happen and a commit is issued immediately. The maximum size of a page blob is 1TB.

    - *Append blob*. These are blocks that are specifically designed for append operations. They do not expose the block ID. When a append blob is modified, blocks are added at the end by the Append Block operation. You cannot update/delete existing blobs. A append blob can be a different size with maximum of 4MB and it can include 50,000 blobs.

Table Storage

Azure table storage contains a large amount of structured non-relational data. Figure 3-2 shows the following key components of a table storage:

- *Storage account*. As discussed earlier, all access to Azure storage is done through the storage accounts.

- Table. A collection of entities that has different sets of properties.

- Entity. Like a row in a database, it is a set of properties that can be up to 1MB size.

- Properties. A name-value pair that can contain around 252 properties to store data.

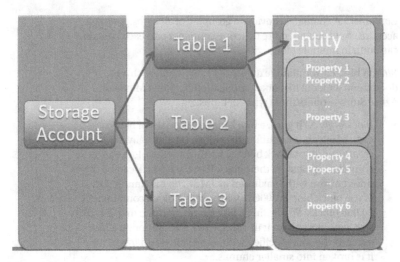

Figure 3-2. *Windows table storage components*

■ **Note**   Refer to https://azure.microsoft.com/en-in/documentation/articles/
storage-dotnet-how-to-use-tables/ to learn how to access table storage using .NET.

Queue Storage

Queue storage is used to store large numbers of messages and can be accessed using
HTTP/HTTPS. It is used to process data asynchronously and it helps in passing messages
between the Azure web role and the Azure worker role.

Queues provide a reliable messaging for your application. They can be used to
perform asynchronous tasks, such as a task from a web role that has to be sent to the
worker role for processing asynchronously. This allows the web and worker role to scale
independently (see Figure 3-3).

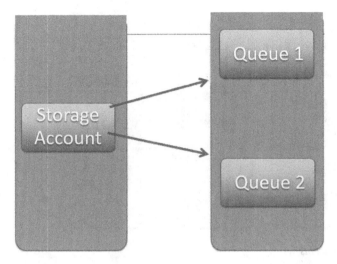

Figure 3-3. *Windows queue storage concepts*

■ **Note** Refer to https://azure.microsoft.com/en-in/documentation/articles/ storage-dotnet-how-to-use-queues/ to learn how to access queue storage using .NET.

File Storage

Many of us still use legacy applications and couldn't function without them. These legacy applications used to use SMB file shares. With the Microsoft Azure file storage service, you get cloud-based SMB file shares, and it can help if you decide to migrate your legacy applications that rely on file shares to Azure. An on-premises application can access data in a file share using the file storage REST API. Common file storage uses include the following:

- Migrating on-premises application that depend on file shares.

- Storing shared application files such as config files.

- Storing diagnostic data such as logs.

- Storing tools and utilities.

If you look at Figure 3-4, you will see that the file service can be used to store the diagnostic logs and application config files. You can create directories and store them at your convenience.

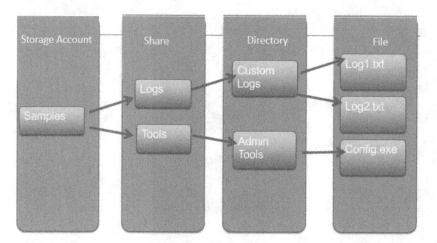

Figure 3-4. *File storage concepts*

■ **Note** For more information, refer to https://azure.microsoft.com/en-in/
documentation/articles/storage-dotnet-how-to-use-files/.

Design Decisions

Microsoft Azure storage was designed based on some key customer engagements:

- *Strong consistency.* For Enterprise customers, consistency is very important in moving their line of business applications to the cloud. It is extremely important for them to perform conditional reads, writes, and deletes for optimistic concurrency control. Microsoft Azure storage thus provides three properties as per the CAP theorem—strong consistency, high availability, and partition tolerance.

- *Global and scalable Namespace storage.* With Microsoft Azure Storage, you can store massive data and access it consistently from anywhere across the globe. Microsoft Azure leverages the DNS as a part of the namespace and breaks the namespace into three parts—a storage account name, a partition name, and an object name (http(s)://AccountName.<Service>.core. windows.net/PartitionName/ObjectName).

- *Disaster recovery.* With Microsoft Azure Storage, the data is stored across multiple data centers that are globally dispersed. This is to ensure that customers' data is protected at any cost against natural disasters like earthquakes, fires, storms, etc.

- *Scalable.* The data needs to be scalable, it should be capable of scaling automatically and be load balanced based on the peak traffic demand.

- *Multi-tenancy.* Many customers, depending on their need, could be served from the same shared storage, thus reducing the cost of storage.

The following are important characteristics of Premium Storage:

- *Durability.* Premium Storage was built on the Locally Redundant Storage (LRS) technology, which stores the replica of data within the same region. This was to confirm durability of data for Enterprise workload. Writes will be confirmed back to the application only when they have been durably replicated by the LRS system.

- *New "DS" series VMs.* The new DS series of Virtual Machines supports Premium Storage data disks. You can leverage a new sophisticated caching capability that enables extremely low latency for read operations.

- *Linux support.* With Linux integration services 4.0, Microsoft have enabled support for even more Linux flavors. There are different distributions that have been validated with Microsoft Azure Premium Storage such as Ubuntu (Versions 12.04, 14.04, 14.10, and 15.04), SUSE 12, etc.

Azure Storage Architecture Internals

A storage stamp is a cluster of racks of storage nodes on Microsoft Azure Fabric where each rack is on a separate domain under redundant networking and power (see Figure 3-5).

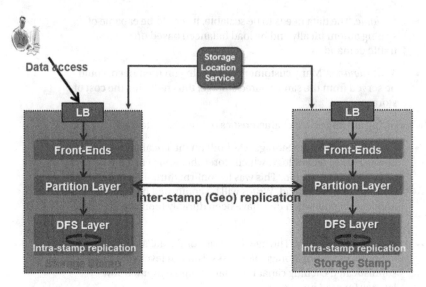

Figure 3-5. *Storage stamps architecture*

All the reads and writes go to these clusters of storage. The target is to keep the storage stamp at about 70% utilized in terms of capacity, transactions, and bandwidth so that better seek time is gained for higher throughput. This provides better resiliency against rack failures within a stamp.

Location Service manages all storage stamps. It does things like account load balancing and account allocation, and it handles geo-replication across these stamps. The location service itself is distributed across two geographic locations for its own disaster recovery.

■ **Note** For more information on Microsoft Azure Storage, we recommend the following sites:

http://sigops.org/sosp/sosp11/current/2011-Cascais/printable/11-calder.pdf

https://blogs.msdn.microsoft.com/windowsazurestorage/2011/11/20/sosp-paper-
windows-azure-storage-a-highly-available-cloud-storage-service-with-strong-
consistency/

Replication Engine

There are two replication engines: intra-stamp replication (stream layer) and inter-stamp replication (partition layer).

Intra-stamp replication provides synchronous replication and ensures all data is durable within the stamp. It keeps different enough copies of data across different fault domains in advent of disk, node, or rack failures. This is done by the partition layer and is in the path of critical path of customer write request. A success is only returned to a client once the data is replicated within an intra-stamp.

Inter-stamp replication provides asynchronous replication by lazily replicating data across the stamps in the background. This is an object-level replication where either whole objects are replicated or the recent changes are. This replication is used to keep data in two locations for disaster recovery, migrating an account's data between stamps. It provides geo-redundancy against geographical disasters by using optimal use of network bandwidth across the stamps.

Layers Within a Storage Stamp

There are three layers within a storage stamp (see Figure 3-6):

- *Stream layer/Distributed File System (DFS) layer.* This is the lowest layer and is responsible for handling the disk and storing data to the disk. This means that it stores the bits on the disk and replicates the data across many servers to keep data durable within a storage stamp. Think of this as a distributed file system layer within a storage stamp. Data is stored into the files, called extents, and they are replicated three times within a region between upgrade domain (UD) and fault domain(FD). This is an append-only filesystem, so data is never overwritten. Data gets appended to the end of the extent.

- *Partition layer.* This serves two unique purposes. This layer understands the data abstractions. It understands what a blob is, what a table entity is, what a message is, and how to perform transactions against those objects. Thus it ensures transaction ordering and optimistic concurrency, storing object data on top of stream layer and caching object data to reduce the disk I/O. This layer is also responsible for partitioning all objects within a stamp. This layer is also responsible for a massively scalable index, this index is used to index all blobs, table entities, and queues. There is a master that's responsible for taking this index and breaking it into range partitions based on the load to the index. These objects are broken into disjointed ranges based on partition name values and served from different partition servers (i.e., it manages which partition server serves which partition range for blobs, tables, and queues). This is done to load-balance the TPS traffic to the big index.

- Front-end layer. Provides a REST protocol for blobs, tables, and queues. It is used for authentication, authorization, and for logging and gathering metrics.

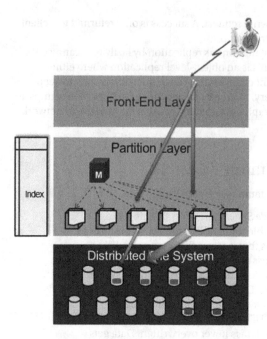

Figure 3-6. *Dynamic load balancing in the partition layer*

You may wonder how this structured storage system is provided in an append-only filesystem, i.e., how only updating blobs/tables is allowed when the filesystem is append only?

At a high level, the data abstractions are treated at the partition layer as logs (streams). Any update to the data is appended to the log, which means that they are appended to the last extent of the logs. Think of this as a list link of extents. Thus, the append happens only to the last extent. All prior extents are sealed and are never appended to those extents. The data is then committed and successfully returned back to the client. In parallel, all the recent updates are stored in memory and in the background, so it would lazily check those off the critical write path. These are then merged to a B-Plus tree. Therefore, there are the logs that are used to commit the updates, and then the checkpoint, and the tree that's used to find the last version of your data.

Maintaining Availability/Consistency for Read Requests

Since all replicas that are maintained bitwise are identical, this implies that they can be read from any replica.

For read availability, parallel read requests are sent out and the first request that comes back is taken and the data is provided to the customers. Now during processing of the read requests if high latency is noticed, in parallel, another read request is issued for it to be processed. The one that returns first will be sent to the client.

Load Balancing of Partition Layer

By load balancing an attempt is made to balance the TPS, i.e., load balance the index. In Figure 3-6, the master continuously monitors the loads to the partition servers as well as to each partition. If it finds one of the partitions to be too hot, which means that this partition is getting far too many requests to be processed, the master can decide quickly to take this range partition and split it into smaller range partitions (one of the ways to deal with such issues).

Once the partition is moved to the different partition server that's comparatively less loaded, it updates the partition map. The front-end can then forward the requests pertaining to the specific range to this new server, which eventually balances the transactions per second. An important part to note is that no data moves (in the DFS layer) during this whole process; it just takes the partition range index and updates it so that the the the partition map knows which partition server to forward the requests to.

Load Balancing of the DFS Layer

For load balancing at the DFS layer, the load is monitored for storage nodes, which is used to determine which replica the data will be read from. In parallel, there is a process to perform the parallel reads in background based on 95% latency.

For writing, the load is monitored for the nodes and the replicas that is being appended to. When some node appears overloaded, it seals the replica and starts appending to a new extent. That's placed at the end of the log.

Load Balancing of DFS Capacity

The replicas are moved around to ensure that all nodes have disks with some free space to be used. The DFS layer is an append only system, which means it would never write anything in place. It is important to have some free space where it would always append. This way hot spots are avoided in storage nodes. In addition, if there is a bad node/disk or if a rack is lost, they have to ensure a faster way to replicate the extents across all nodes/disks. With available disk space, this can be done quickly.

Durability Offerings with Azure Storage

There are three types of durability offered with Azure Storage.

- *LRS (Local Redundant Storage)*. Stores three replicas of data within a single zone in a single region. All the three replicas will be in the same zone, thus providing durability despite node/rack/disk failure.

- *ZRS (Zone Redundant Storage)*. Available for block blobs and stores three replicas of data across multiple zones and is designed to keep all three replicas in the same region, but not mandatory as sometimes you might just store it in different region as well. In addition to this, it provides durability over LRS as now the data is durable against zone-related failures (such as a fire in a facility in a zone).

- *GRS (Globally Redundant Storage)*. You store six replicas, three in the primary region and three in the secondary region, geographically dispersed. This provides additional durability to protect data against major regional catastrophic disaster(s), such as storms, tornados, earthquakes, or hurricanes.

Azure Premium Storage

Azure Premium Storage was introduced by Microsoft. It helps deliver high-performance, low-latency disk support for virtual machines running I/O-intensive workloads. It uses SSD (solid state drives) to store the data. If your workload needs high throughput and you want to take advantage of the speed and performance of these disks, Premium Storage should be your choice.

For Azure Virtual Machine workloads that need consistent high IO performance and low latency, Premium Storage is appropriate. In order to host IO intensive workloads like OLTP, Big Data, and Data Warehousing on platforms like SQL Server, MongoDB, Cassandra, and others, Premium Storage is a good choice.

With Premium Storage, your application can store up to 64TB of data per VM and can give you throughput of 80Kbps IOPs (Input Output Operations per Second) per VM and 2000Mbps disk throughput per VM.

There are quite a few points you need to keep in mind in order to use Premium Storage:

- You need a Premium Storage account. Premium Storage accounts can be created using storage REST APIs version 2014-02-14 or later (Storage and Service Management), PowerShell 8.10 or later, or the Ibiza portal (https://portal.azure.com). When you create a Premium Storage account using PowerShell, you need to specify the type parameter as Premium_LRS. For example: New-AzureStorageAccount -StorageAccountName "Testpremiumaccount" - Location "East US" -Type "Premium_LRS".

- Not all regions support Premium Storage. Currently, the Central US, East and West US, Northern and Western Europe, East and West Japan, Southeast Asia, and Eastern Australia support it.

- It only supports Azure page blobs, as it is used to hold persistent disks that can be used for Azure Virtual Machines.

- It is locally redundant and keeps three copies of data in same region.

- In order to use Premium Storage, you need to provision either GS-series or DS-series of VMs.

- For all Premium data disks, the default disk caching policy is read-only and Premium operating system disks attached to the VM are set to read-write.

- For Premium Storage accounts, the IOPs depends on the size of the disk. At present there are three types of premium disks—P10, P20, and P30. See Table 3-1 for IOPs and throughput specifications.

Table 3-1. Premium Disk Storage limits

Disk Type	P10	P20	P30
Disk size	128GB	512GB	1TB
IOPS (per disk)	500	2300	5000
Throughput (per disk)	100Mbps	150Mbps	200Mbps

Using PowerShell, you can create a VM using Premium Storage. The following code snippets/cmdlets can be used to try this out. Note they are just cmdlets and should be used as such. There are MSDN links that you can refer to as well; see https://msdn.microsoft.com/en-us/library/mt607148.aspx.

Creating an Azure VM Machine Using Premium Storage and PowerShell

Create the following Premium Storage account:

```
C:\> New-AzureRmStorageAccount -ResourceGroupName "TestResourceGroup"
-AccountName "TestStorageAccount" -Location "US East" -Type "Premium_LRS"
```

The following code only uses ARM cmdlet; it can be used to create a VM:

```
# Set values for existing resource group and storage account names
$rgName="RGServers"
$locName="East US"
$saName="Testserverssa"

# Set the existing virtual network and subnet index
$vnetName="XYZ"
$subnetIndex=0
$vnet=Get-AzureRmVirtualNetwork -Name $vnetName -ResourceGroupName $rgName

# Create the NIC
$nicName="Test-NIC"
$domName="TestDom"
$pip=New-AzureRmPublicIpAddress -Name $nicName -ResourceGroupName $rgName
-DomainNameLabel $domName -Location $locName -AllocationMethod Dynamic
```

```
$nic=New-AzureRmNetworkInterface -Name $nicName -ResourceGroupName
$rgName -Location $locName -SubnetId $vnet.Subnets[$subnetIndex].Id
-PublicIpAddressId $pip.Id

# Specify the name, size, and existing availability set
$vmName="TestVM"
$vmSize="Standard_A3"
$avName="Test_AS"
$avSet=Get-AzureRmAvailabilitySet –Name $avName –ResourceGroupName $rgName
$vm=New-AzureRmVMConfig -VMName $vmName -VMSize $vmSize -AvailabilitySetId
$avset.Id

# Add 200GB data disk
$diskSize=200
$diskLabel="TestStorage"
$diskName="Test-DISK01"
$storageAcc=Get-AzureRmStorageAccount -ResourceGroupName $rgName -Name $saName
$vhdURI=$storageAcc.PrimaryEndpoints.Blob.ToString() + "vhds/" + $vmName +
$diskName + ".vhd"
Add-AzureRmVMDataDisk -VM $vm -Name $diskLabel -DiskSizeInGB $diskSize
-VhdUri $vhdURI -CreateOption empty

# Specify the image and local administrator account, and then add the NIC
$pubName="MicrosoftWindowsServer"
$offerName="WindowsServer"
$skuName="2012-R2-Datacenter"
$cred=Get-Credential -Message "Type the name and password of the local
administrator account."
$vm=Set-AzureRmVMOperatingSystem -VM $vm -Windows -ComputerName $vmName
-Credential $cred -ProvisionVMAgent -EnableAutoUpdate
$vm=Set-AzureRmVMSourceImage -VM $vm -PublisherName $pubName -Offer
$offerName -Skus $skuName -Version "latest"
$vm=Add-AzureRmVMNetworkInterface -VM $vm -Id $nic.Id

# Specify the OS disk name and create the VM
$diskName="OSDisk"
$storageAcc=Get-AzureRmStorageAccount -ResourceGroupName $rgName -Name $saName
$osDiskUri=$storageAcc.PrimaryEndpoints.Blob.ToString() + "vhds/" + $vmName
+ $diskName + ".vhd"
$vm=Set-AzureRmVMOSDisk -VM $vm -Name $diskName -VhdUri $osDiskUri
-CreateOption fromImage
New-AzureRmVM -ResourceGroupName $rgName -Location $locName -VM $vm
Ref: https://azure.microsoft.com/en-in/documentation/articles/virtual-
machines-windows-create-powershell/
```

Inside Premium Storage

Premium Storage disks are implemented as page blobs in Azure storage. Every uncached write operation replicates to the SSDs as three servers in different racks (fault domains). The data in Premium Storage is stored on SSD drives, thereby providing higher throughput. The disk used are different than the ones you would get using Standard Storage. There is a component called blob cache that runs on the servers, hosting these VMs and taking advantage of the RAM/SSDs of the servers to implement higher throughput and low latency. It is enabled for both premium and standard disks and is configured with read-only and read-write caching. For read-only caching, it synchronously writes data to the cache and to Azure Storage. For write-caching enabled disks, it would write data back to Azure Storage when a VM requests it. This is done through disk flush or by specifying the write through flags on an I/O (forced unit access).

The VMs can take advantage of this caching architecture and can provide extremely high throughput and low latency, thereby boosting performance tremendously.

Azure Storage Best Practices

It is important for all developers to build their applications using best practices. Experience from customer engagement has led us to some key lessons while dealing with Azure storage and getting the maximum performance out of it.

Performance Enhancement Using Blobs

Performance is important when you deal with any form of application, let alone blobs. This section looks at a few of the important points to keep in mind when you're working with blobs. When you store files in blobs and you read and write to and from blobs, there are few key aspects to keep in mind.

A single blob can be read and written at up to a maximum of 60Mbps and a single blob supports up to 500 requests per second. If you have multiple clients that need to read the same blob and you might exceed these limits, you should consider using a CDN for distributing the blob.

Try to match your read size with your write size and avoid reading small ranges from blobs with large blocks. The following properties are used to control read and write size: `CloudBlockBlob.StreamMinimumReadSizeInBytes` and `StreamWriteSizeInBytes`.

You can upload folder contents by uploading multiple files in parallel or by uploading concurrently. Uploading concurrently means multiple workers upload different blobs. Uploading in parallel means multiple workers upload different blocks of the same blob.

Uploading multiple blobs concurrently will execute faster than uploading multiple blob blocks to the same blob. This is because uploading multiple blob blocks to a single blob in parallel affects a single partition and will be limited by the partition performance targets. Uploading multiple blobs in parallel will work on many different partitions and will probably be limited by the Virtual Machines' bandwidth.

Copy/Move Blobs

You can use storage REST APIs to copy blobs across storage accounts. A client application can instruct the storage service to copy a blob from any other storage account. The copy can happen asynchronously, which reduces the bandwidth. However, you need to be careful with asynchronous processes, as there is no completion time guarantee. It is better to download the blob to the VM and then copy it to the destination. During copying, you need to ensure that the VM is in the same region.

AzCopy

This utility released by the storage team can be used to transfer the blobs to and from the storage accounts. The transfer rate that you get is very high and it is recommended you use this for bulk uploads, downloads, and other copy scenarios. (See https://azure. microsoft.com/en-us/documentation/articles/storage-use-azcopy/ for more information.)

Choosing the Right Kind of Blob

Azure Storage supports two types of blobs—*page* blobs and *block* blobs. You need to choose the right kind of blob based on the use-case scenario as this can largely impact the performance and scalability. Block blobs are appropriate when you want to upload large amounts of data such as to upload photos or video to blob storage. Page blobs are appropriate if the application needs to perform random writes on the data.

Use the following URL as a checklist when you're working with Microsoft Azure Storage. Application developers can follow the article, which is comprehensive with important practices documented. It will help in boosting performance of the application. See https://azure.microsoft.com/en-us/documentation/articles/storage-performance-checklist/.

Performance Enhancement Using Tables

The following list provides a few tips for working with tables, which is another service that can be used effectively in different scenarios, as discussed in this chapter.

- *Scalability*. The system usually performs load balancing as your traffic increases, but if your traffic has sudden bursts, you may not be able to get this volume of throughput immediately. If your pattern has bursts, you should expect to see throttling and/or timeouts during the burst as the storage service automatically load balances your table. The recommendation is to slowly ramp up, which gives the system time to load balance appropriately.

- *JSON (Java Script Object Notation).* A popular and concise format for REST protocol. OData supports AtomPub and JSON. A drawback of Atom is its verbose nature, which you may not need when you are writing a table service. The table service supports JSON instead of the XML-based AtomPub format for transferring table data. This can reduce payload sizes by as much as 75% and can significantly improve the performance of your application.

- *Naggle off.* Nagle's algorithm is very popular and is implemented across TCP/IP networks to improve network performance. This may not give you optimal performance specifically in some very high interactive systems. For Azure Storage, Nagle's algorithm has a negative impact on the performance of requests to the table and queue services, and you should disable it if possible.

- *Tables and partitions.* It is very important how you represent your data, as that has a huge impact on the performance of the table service. Tables are divided into partitions. Every entity stored in a partition shares the same partition key and has a unique row key to identify it within that partition. The benefit is that you can update the entities in a single transaction, up to 100 separate storage operations. You can also query data within a single partition more efficiently than data that spans partitions. Partition supports atomic batch transactions and thus the access to entities stored in a single partition cannot be load balanced. Thus as a developer you should use the following techniques:

  - Data that your client application frequently updates or queries should be in the same partition. This may be because your application is aggregating writes, or because you want to take advantage of atomic batch operations.

  - Data that your client application does not frequently update/query in the same atomic transaction should be in separate partitions.

  - Avoid hot partitions, which are partitions that receive more data as compared to the other partitions. If the partitioning scheme results in a single partition that has data that's used far more often than in the other partitions, expect to see throttling. It is likely that the partition will approach the scalability target. It is better to make sure that your partition scheme results in no single partition approaching the scalability target.

Once you store data in the Microsoft Azure Storage Services, it is important that you understand the best practices that can help you retrieve your data. The next section covers these important practices.

Querying Data Best Practices

Once you store data in Microsoft Azure Storage Services, it is important that you understand the best practices that can help you retrieve the data.

As a best practice for querying data, a general rule of thumb is to avoid scans. Now if you have to do scans, you should organize the data so that the unnecessary data scans can be avoided.

- *Point queries.* Try to use these types of queries as much as possible as they return only one entity by specifying the partition key and the row key.

- *Partition query.* These queries are less performant than point queries and should be used carefully. They retrieve sets of data that share common partition keys and typically you specify a range of row key values or a range of values for some entity property in addition to a partition key.

- *Table queries.* This is a query that retrieves a set of entities that do not share a common partition key and are not efficient and should be avoided as much as possible.

- Query density. One of the important factors in efficiency of a query performance is the number of entities returned and the number of entities scanned. A low query density can cause the table service to throttle your application and so should be avoided. The following are some ways that you can avoid them:

  - Filter the data so that the query returns only data that your application will consume. The performance of your application will increase due to less network payload and fewer entities that your application must process.

  - Use projection to limit the size of returned data set that your client application needs.

  - Remove redundant data (denormalize). This has always been helpful as it minimizes the number of entities that a query must scan to find the data the client needs, rather than having to scan large numbers of entities to find the data your application needs.

Summary

Microsoft Azure Storage services has all that an application developer needs to provide a robust, scalable cloud-based solution. With its many useful features, it provides the best platform to host your application and store the data securely. You need not think about the DR strategy, as it's all taken care of. Now with the Premium Storage offering, the throughput increases and you get a tremendous boost on application performance.

CHAPTER 4

■ ■ ■

Microsoft Azure Networking

With the help of Microsoft Azure, you can create Virtual Machines that run within Microsoft data centers. These virtual machines that you create eventually form a part of a workgroup. Traditionally, you can have an application hosted on your virtual machine and the data could reside on SQL Server, which could be on a different virtual machine. These machines need to talk to each other, so you not only need to connect, you also need to communicate between them. In order to connect from the application, you can use SQL Authentication or a pass-through Windows authentication to connect to SQL Server since these machines resides on a workgroup.

There are different data centers spread across the globe where different customers and businesses run in Microsoft Azure. It provides the perfect platform to host your business in cloud and reduce the TCO. Thus in order to have your business hosted in Microsoft Azure or store data, you can use one of these data centers spread across globe.

As shown in Figure 4-1, you can connect to these data centers in three different ways:

- Connect the on-premises network to a separate network that has set of virtual machines.

- Use *Azure AD Connect to link the Microsoft Azure application to the on-premises Windows servers.

    See https://azure.microsoft.com/en-in/documentation/articles/active-directory-aadconnect/.

- Use Microsoft Azure Traffic Manager to route requests to multiple data centers where the different instances of the Microsoft Azure application run.

© Pranab Mazumdar, Sourabh Agarwal, Amit Banerjee 2016
P. Mazumdar et al., *Pro SQL Server on Microsoft Azure*, DOI 10.1007/978-1-4842-2083-2_4

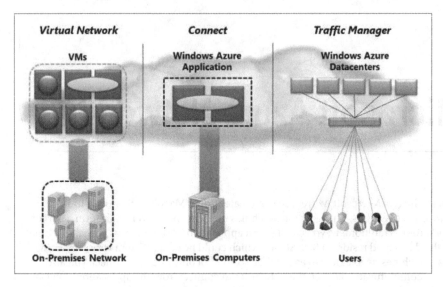

Figure 4-1. *Typical setups using different components*

You can also create Virtual Networks in the cloud. You could create your test environment in Microsoft Azure with a domain controller (DC) for user authentication, and you can host your application servers. Your data resides in SQL Servers which is provisioned in Microsoft Azure, which utilizes the massively scalable, highly secure Microsoft Azure storage. You need to create a Virtual Network to configure secure site-to-site connectivity as well as protected private Virtual Network in the cloud. Thus you can build your complete office network within Microsoft Azure.

In this chapter, you'll see how Microsoft Azure allows you to create a VPN and allows your on-premise networks to connect and talk to each other. You can also connect Azure applications on-premises as well as distribute load across different data centers. You will also be introduced to a few key networking components/concepts, which you can study further if you are interested.

Networking Primer

Connecting your on-premise securely to a Virtual Network can help in expanding your business and reduce cost by leveraging the Microsoft Azure Services. There are at least three options that could help you connect and expand your hybrid network: Site-to-Site, Point-to-Site, and ExpressRoute. See Figure 4-2 and Table 4-1 for more detail.

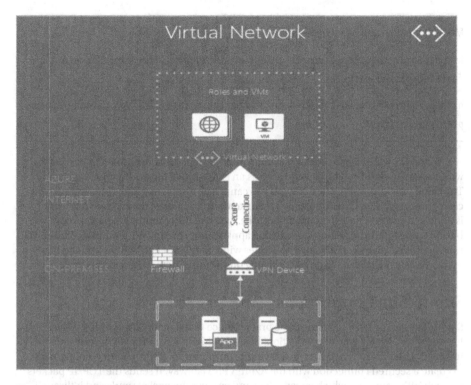

Figure 4-2. *Typical hybrid setup*

Table 4-1. *Choosing the Best Connectivity Options*

	Point-to-Site	**Site-to-Site**	**ExpressRoute**
Azure Services	Cloud Service and Virtual Machine	Cloud Service and Virtual Machine	Most services, Refer to the link in PS
Bandwidth	Less than 100MBPS	Less than 100MBPS	50MBPS-10GBPS
Supported Protocols	Secure Socket Tunneling Protocol (SSTP)	IPSec	Direct connections over VLANs, NSPs, and VPN technologies
Connection Resiliency	Active–Passive	Active–Passive	Active–Active

Before you opt for one of these options, you should consider few points, such as the following questions. How much throughput does your application require? Does your application connect via a public Internet? Do you have a public IP available? Do you need VPN gateways?

More information can be found here:

https://azure.microsoft.com/en-in/documentation/articles/expressroute-faqs/#supported-services

https://azure.microsoft.com/en-in/documentation/articles/vpn-gateway-cross-premises-options/

In today's world where businesses span multiple regions across different parts of the world, a public cloud can be cleverly used as an extension of the on-Premise data center. The cloud provides you the flexibility as you can create virtual machines on demand, you can pause/stop them if you don't need them, and you can delete them once your work is done and you don't need them anymore, i.e., you use the compute whenever your business needs it. In addition, your existing applications running on-premises continue to run smoothly. You can spin Virtual Machines with SharePoint and SQL Server, and have an Active Directory that can talk to your existing on-premises Active Directory as well.

Site-to-Site Connections

Site-to-Site can be used to connect the branch office to the main office, which is the headquarters. In this type of connection, hosts would not have VPN client software installed. The VPN device that is located in the on-premises environment is configured to create a secured connection with the Azure VPN Gateway. It sends the TCP/IP packets through VPN gateways, which encapsulate and encrypt the packets and send it through the VPN tunnel. There is then a VPN gateway at the destination that receives the packets, deciphers the header and the content from the packet, and then sends the same to the destination host.

The following describe a few scenarios when you would use the Site-to-Site connections:

- For creating a hybrid solution.

- The requirement for the business is a consistent and reliable network connection.

- You don't need any client-side configuration for connecting your on-premises network to your VPN.

The requirement for setting up a Site-to-Site connections is primarily that you need a compatible VPN device having an Internet-facing IP address. This device should be compatible with the VPN gateway type.

Point-to-Site Connections

You can use this to create a secure connection to your Virtual Network. Unlike with Site-to-Site, you need to install a VPN client and configure it on every client that intends to connect to the Virtual Network. You also don't need a VPN device with an Internet-facing IP address.

The following describes a few scenarios when you would use the Point-to-Site connections:

- You have a handful of clients who want to connect to the Virtual Network.

- Remote connectivity is a requirement by your clients.

- There is an existing Site-to-Site connection; however, a few clients have to connect to the Virtual Network from a remote location.

Virtual Networks provide you with an option to create a private network within Azure. Using this, different services can talk to each other or to on-premises resources.

This concept is quite interesting and useful as well; however, in order to make it beneficial, the users should treat the applications as if it were running on their own on-premises data center. Your network administrator can set up a Microsoft Azure Virtual Private Network between your local on-premises network and Microsoft Azure, where multiple Virtual Machines can run. This can be done with the help of a VPN gateway device. You can choose your own IP v4 address and assign it to these Virtual Machines that run in the cloud VMs. This means it would appear that this is an extension of your existing network. The end users would be able to access the application running on those Virtual Machines seamlessly, as if they were accessing them on their local network.

ExpressRoute

ExpressRoute is a pretty neat concept, whereby you get your own private connection to Azure. ExpressRoute is a connection that bypasses the public Internet that connects your on-premises infrastructure to Microsoft Azure data centers (see Figure 4-3). This helps Azure act like your own private cloud.

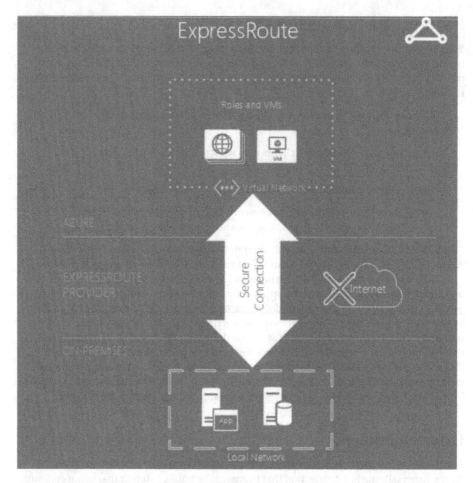

Figure 4-3. Hybrid setup with ExpressRoute

There are two ways to establish your private connections to Microsoft Azure. The first way is to connect through a exchange provider facility; if you are using a exchange provider facility, you could directly connect to the Azure. Alternatively, you can establish a direct connection through your network service provider between the on-premises site and the Microsoft Azure data center.

Microsoft Azure would appear as just another site on your WAN. ExpressRoute is seamless and it works great with all sorts of technology. It also provides built-in redundancy. Microsoft works directly with your network service provider. It delivers throughput that is faster, nearly 10Gbps. Thus, with ExpressRoute you have your network infrastructure superbly secured, with low latency, high throughput and great reliability. If you use ExpressRoute for data transfer between on-premises and the Microsoft Azure data center, you can enjoy cost benefits as well. Since it is fast and reliable, it can be used for data migration, replication for business continuity, disaster recovery, and high-availability strategies.

With ExpressRoute, you can leverage the compute and storage capacity of Microsoft Azure and add that to your existing data centers. Since it is reliable and offers high throughput connections, you could build a hybrid application that expands from your existing data center through the Microsoft Azure data center. Interestingly, you get all of this without compromising on security or performance.

Azure AD Connect

Using Azure AD Connect, you can connect your on-premises identity infrastructure to the active directory hosted in Microsoft Azure. It presents you with a wizard that guides you with the prerequisites and the components needed for the connection. Using this tool, you can configure common identity for your users for Office 365, Azure, and SaaS applications, which are integrated along with Azure AD. When you install the tool, it installs the prerequisites like .NET Framework, Azure Active Directory, the PowerShell module, and the Microsoft Online Service assistant for sign-in. It configures sync for one of the multiple active directory forests. It also helps you configure password hash sync or Active Directory Federation with a web application. You can read more about it at https://azure.microsoft.com/en-in/documentation/articles/active-directory-aadconnect/.

Traffic Manager

In today's world where users are spread around the globe, the challenge is running an application instance in multiple data centers. The main challenge is how to intelligently redirect the traffic to the application instances running in the dispersed data centers. The aim is usually to assign users access to the application that's running in closest proximity to them, in order to get the best response time and throughput.

Traffic Manager helps you control the distribution of the traffic and route it to specific end points like website, cloud services, etc. Basically, you define rules that determine how the traffic will be routed/distributed to the data centers for the Traffic Manager to follow. For example, usually the request could be routed to the closest data center from the user location; however, it's not always true that the response time from that data center will be best. In such cases, users could be routed to other data centers. This type of service is very useful in modern-day business, where your users are spread across the planet.

The following are the main benefits that Traffic Manager provides:

- It helps improve availability of mission-critical applications.

- You get better response time for high-performant applications.

- You could perform application upgrades by disabling your endpoints and enable the same once the service is complete.

- Finally, you can specify an endpoint to another Traffic Manager, thereby distributing complex application deployments.

Figure 4-4 shows how the rules enable Traffic Manager to route global traffic.

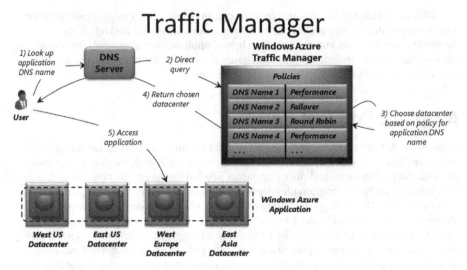

Figure 4-4. *Traffic Manager workflow*

Virtual Private Network

In today's world, most organizations opt for a hybrid kind of a scenario, putting their data in the cloud as well as in an on-premises data center. For example, you could create a Virtual Private Network (VPN) and link your cloud environment to the branch office (see Figure 4-5).

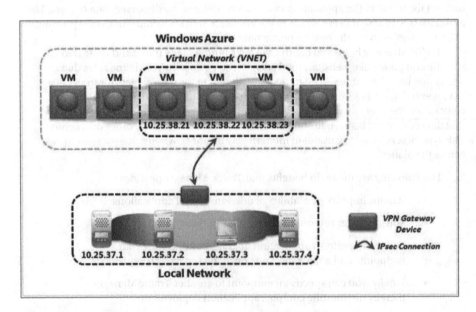

Figure 4-5. *Typical VPN setup*

Using Microsoft Azure Virtual Network, you can create a logical boundary by grouping the virtual machines together, called Virtual Network or VNet. Once the VNet is set up, you can establish a IPsec connection between your local on-premises data center and the VNet. This, however, is not needed for ExpressRoute setup. You can create the virtual machines in the Virtual Network by using the Microsoft Azure VMs or Microsoft Azure Cloud Services, or both. You could choose the IaaS or the PaaS service offering from Microsoft Azure to create Virtual Machines or services. When you create the IPsec connection, it basically requires the following:

- You need a virtual private network (VPN) gateway device.

- You need specialized hardware that will be connected to your on-premises network.

- You need a network administrator who will help set this up for you.

Once this network and setup is ready, the virtual machines running within the VNet will appear as an extension of your on-premises network.

Notice that the IP addresses in Figure 4-5 are allocated from the same IP address range that is available for your on-premises local network. The software that runs on the local network will be able to see the Virtual Machines as if they were available within their own on-premises local network. It is interesting to note that the physical machines that host these Virtual Machines on either side of the network could run any operating system, as the connection happens at the IP layer and is thus transparent. For example, the Microsoft Azure VMs running a Linux operating system can talk to your on-premise machines that run Windows or vice versa. You can use the infrastructure tools like SCCM to manage the cloud's Virtual Machines.

A very important aspect of having such an expanded network is that you can easily extend your existing on-premises active directory domain to the Microsoft Azure Virtual Network and give users single sign-in so that they can run applications from anywhere. If need be, you could have a domain created in the Microsoft Azure cloud and connect it to your existing on-premises domain. As your Virtual Network is an extension of your on-premises network, the reverse is also true.

You could technically use the software running in your local network from your Microsoft Azure Network as well. If you prefer to keep your data local for privacy reasons, such as many hospitals and medical facilities do, you can use this concept of the Virtual Network and expand your network so that the data remains in your on-premises network (stored locally) and yet the users can access the data from application instances running across multiple data centers in Microsoft Azure.

This gives you the flexibility to access a large pool of resources as per your needs. Elasticity in the cloud space is a great concept and directly impacts your financials, as it reduces the total cost of ownership. You can spin a Virtual Machine when you need it and upon completion just remove/release the resource (virtual machine in this context). You will only be charged for the period that you used them. Imagine you have a request to get a machine ready and the requirement is urgent. Using Microsoft Azure, you could set up the Virtual Machine in no time and you are all set in few minutes.

Load Balancer

Using Azure Load Balancer, you get high availability and a boost to your network applications. It balances and spreads out the load using layer 4 TCP/UDP load balancer and distributes it through different, healthy services. Load balancing is accomplished using endpoints, which have a one-to-many relationship between the public IP and the local ports that are assigned to the virtual machines where the load will be eventually distributed. Here are a few of the scenarios when using Load Balancer is a good idea:

- It would load balance Internet traffic to Virtual Machines.

- It can also load balance the incoming traffic between the Virtual Machines within the Virtual Network. It can be Used To Distribute the load between different virtual machines within a cloud service.

- It can also forward external traffic to a specific Virtual Machine.

Azure DNS

Any service or website will be associated with a IP address. Domain Naming System (DNS) helps translate the IP address to user-friendly names for the service or website.

Azure DNS provides name resolution using the Microsoft Azure infrastructure. You can host your domains within Microsoft Azure data centers and yet manage your DNS records using the same credentials that you have been using. DNS domains within Azure DNS are hosted within the global DNS network name servers. This service provides faster performance and high availability for your domains. You need to purchase the domains from a third-party registrar and then they can be hosted in Azure DNS for managing DNS records.

Summary

Microsoft Azure allows you to create a VPN and allows your on-premises network connections to talk to each other. You can connect an Azure application on-premises as well as distribute loads across different data centers. You can extend your existing business with minimal impact and save a lot of money. Be sure to go through the references at the end of the chapter, which are a part of the rich Azure documentation.

Additional References

- https://azure.microsoft.com/en-us/documentation/ articles/fundamentals-introduction-to-azure/#networking

- https://azure.microsoft.com/en-us/documentation/ articles/active-directory-aadconnect/

CHAPTER 5

■ ■ ■

Deploying SQL Server on Azure VMs

Over the years, automation has grown from batch files to PowerShell and finally automation routines. With the advent of the cloud, the word "automation" took on a whole new meaning. Whether you deployed in a public or private cloud, the mass scale that was required to perform the deployment could not be satisfied by any staffing model. The industry saw an immense need for automating the repetitive tasks, monitoring the deployed services and providing insights on the artifacts associated with your deployment. The word "scale-up" and "scale-out" in a cloud environment cannot be de-coupled without automation.

In the Microsoft Azure environment, you have workflows available that allow you to specify inputs, which the workflow will use as parameters to deploy the virtual machine with your required settings. In the traditional world of IT, a SQL Server deployment would have prerequisites like procuring hardware, setting up the hardware and the operating system, and then getting the prerequisites fulfilled like IP addresses, permissions, etc. After all these prerequisites were done, you would need to get the SQL Server installation media, run the installation with the necessary parameters, and then perform post-installation configuration steps.

A large number of IT professionals around the world leveraged various scripting and automation methods to make these deployments faster. A number of environments moved to virtualization to make the deployment of these environments quicker and lessen the procurement timeframe. If you were a firm believer that virtualization led to cost savings and prevented underutilization of resources, the cloud takes that a step further. It is truly like a pre-paid cellular service! You only pay for what you use. This pay-as-you-go model is replicated in many shared services models within enterprises in the form of charge back to a cost center. In this chapter, we will draw parallels of deployment with the on-premises world in Azure and explain the different deployment options present for SQL Server instances hosted on Azure VMs.

© Pranab Mazumdar, Sourabh Agarwal, Amit Banerjee 2016
P. Mazumdar et al., *Pro SQL Server on Microsoft Azure*, DOI 10.1007/978-1-4842-2083-2_5

Deploying a Standalone SQL Server Instance

In the previous chapters, the Azure architecture was explained in detail along with the deployment models (Classic and ARM) available in Azure. Since Azure is transitioning to the Resource Manager (ARM) deployment model, this chapter will focus only on this particular model. When you log onto the Azure portal (portal.azure.com), you will be presented with a column view on the left that allows you to look at the various artifacts deployed and also the services that can be deployed.

One of the most common questions is why do you see two different items for Virtual Machines (see Figure 5-1). The Virtual Machines option is for virtual machines deployed using the Resource Manager model and the Virtual Machines (Classic) option is for virtual machines deployed using the Classic deployment model. The old portal (manage.windowsazure.com) does not show virtual machines deployed using the Resource Manager model.

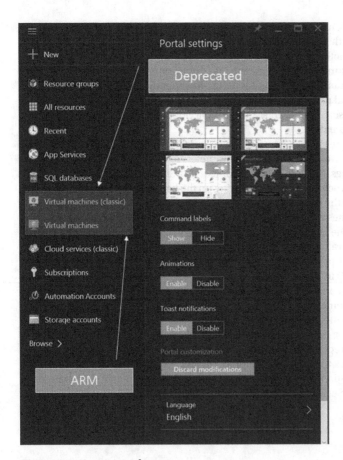

Figure 5-1. *Azure portal*

Now that you are aware of the navigation differences, let us break the journey of deploying SQL Server into different phases. The first phase of the journey is choosing the deployment. Azure Virtual Machines provide multiple choices for deployment for SQL Server from a licensing perspective.

- Deploying a SQL Server image from the marketplace (see Figure 5-2) and paying the per-minute rate of SQL Server

- Installing or uploading your own SQL Server image using License Mobility benefits under Software Assurance

- As a Service Provider with a Services Provider License Agreement (SPLA), you have an additional option of using your own image with Subscriber Access License (SAL) reported via your SPLA

Configuration Settings

Figure 5-2 shows the marketplace browsing options for Compute when you click on New option available on the left corner of the homepage. The marketplace allows you to deploy SQL Server releases ranging from SQL Server 2008 R2 to SQL Server 2016. You can even choose a range of editions like Enterprise, Standard, and Express. Another option is to pick pre-canned solutions like Availability Group deployment templates, which allow you to deploy Availability Groups during deployment.

Figure 5-2. *Azure Marketplace image showing SQL Server 2016 3.3 image*

Virtual Machine Region

For certain compute deployment options, you can select the deployment model (Classic or ARM). Once you select the image that you want to deploy, you will be provided with a number of options to specify the virtual machine and SQL Server settings (if you are using a SQL Server image). This part of the journey is where you provide inputs to the Azure deployment workflow for configuring various options for your environment. These options are constantly being reviewed by the Microsoft Engineering teams. Enhancements and improvements to these options are added during the sprint releases based on user inputs and available telemetry. Once you start working with the cloud, you learn that the public cloud is like the weather. You know the seasons and can sort of predict the weather based on various signs, but you will be pleasantly surprised once in a while. The only difference with the weather is that the enhancements and improvements showing up in various workflows are to make your life easier rather than more difficult. The Cloud Engineering teams are one of the most agile development organizations within Microsoft.

The Basics settings view showing Figure 5-3 are common to all Azure Virtual Machine configuration wizards and they allow you to specify the machine name, administrator username, password, and resource group name (since we are using ARM). You also have the option to specify the region, i.e., the data center where this virtual machine will be deployed, and the subscription. These are very important things to consider, as these cannot be changed using the portal after the deployment has completed. If you want to move an existing Azure Virtual Machine to a different region or subscription, you will need to write PowerShell commands to get this done. This is not something that happens in the blink of an eye!

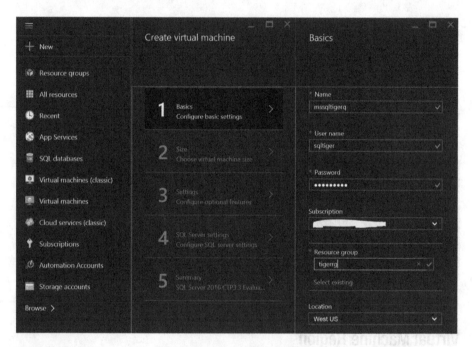

Figure 5-3. Basic settings configuration for Azure Virtual Machine

Picking a subscription is an easier consideration. You would want to pick the subscription that should get billed for the resource usage and that would typically host the other parts of your application. This decision does not have performance considerations associated with it. However, picking the region for the virtual machine has performance aspects associated with it. The easiest way to think about the region is your data center. For a production environment, you would pick the server blades and SAN which are colocated within the same data center. Additionally, you would deploy your application in the same data center as well preferably unless you have geo-dispersed requirement. The same logic applies here. You would pick the same region for your compute, storage, and application deployment. This would prevent network hops across data centers, which would increase latency and negatively impact performance. This is one of the most common deployment misconfigurations that have been noticed in multitier architectures using Azure Virtual Machines.

Virtual Machine Hardware

The next set of inputs is also critical for performance and achieving the SLA that your application is supposed to adhere to. This involves choosing the right compute tier for your virtual machine. Figure 5-4 shows the different options that Azure provides. For critical production environments, the recommendation is to pick a compute tier that provides SSD disks (premium storage). The wizard would provide the CPU cores and RAM that is associated with each tier that you pick. Think of the size setting as picking your hardware but without the hassle of understanding the underlying configuration of hardware. All you need to know is the amount of horsepower (processing, IOPs, and physical memory) that your application database needs to run.

Figure 5-4. *Picking the Azure Virtual Machine size*

A major pitfall in this configuration is that most people forget to estimate the IOPs correctly during configuration. Azure will throttle IO bursts if they exceed the virtual machine or storage account's maximum published limits (see Figure 5-5). This can lead to erratic performance slowdown in your virtual machine and thereby negatively impact user experience. Azure provides monitoring endpoints that can be used to determine if existing storage limits are being exceeded. You can even set up alerts to get notified when a threshold is exceeded. Chapter 7 covers more details about performance aspects for SQL Server instances running on Azure Virtual Machines.

Virtual machine disks: per disk limits

VM Tier	Basic Tier VM	Standard Tier VM
Disk size	1023 GB	1023 GB
Max 8 KB IOPS per persistent disk	300	500
Max number of highly utilized disks	66	40

Figure 5-5. *Azure Standard storage account limits*

Once you select the desired size, you will be provided with a number of knobs that allow you to configure the storage account. At the time of going to print, the Azure Storage limits were 100 storage accounts per subscription, with a limit of 500TB per Standard storage account. The maximum size of a page blob is 1TB, which means that the maximum size of a virtual hard disk attached to your virtual machine is 1TB. Depending on the virtual machine tier that you select, your storage size will be limited. In Figure 5-4, the selection of a DS4 standard would limit your storage to a maximum of 16 data disks, which means a storage size limit of 16TB. Furthermore, you need to keep in mind that each storage disk has a limit for the maximum IOPs supported for 8KB IOPs. For a standard tier virtual machine, it is limited to 500.

The calculation for the number of disks required for Standard and Premium storage is shown here.

```
Number of disks required:
For Standard Storage = MAX of [(Total storage required (in GB) ÷ 1024),
(Total IOPs required ÷ 500)]

For Premium Storage (P30) = MAX of [Total storage required (in GB) ÷ 1024),
(Total IOPs required ÷ 5000), (Total MB/s of IO required ÷ 200)]
```

If we had to put things into perspective, if you required 1TB of storage that supported 2000 IOPs, you would need four data disks, which would be hitting the scalability limit. If you were using P30 premium storage, you would be able to utilize a single premium IO disk and still have some room for additional luggage (see Figure 5-6).

Virtual machine disks: per account limits

Resource	Default Limit
Total disk capacity per account	35 TB
Total snapshot capacity per account	10 TB
Max bandwidth per account (ingress + egress[1])	<=50 Gbps

[1]*Ingress* refers to all data (requests) being sent to a storage account. *Egress* refers to all data (responses) being received from a storage account.

Virtual machine disks: per disk limits

Premium Storage Disk Type	P10	P20	P30
Disk size	128 GiB	512 GiB	1024 GiB (1 TB)
Max IOPS per disk	500	2300	5000
Max throughput per disk	100 MB per second	150 MB per second	200 MB per second
Max number of highly utilized disks	62	41	31

Figure 5-6. *Azure Premium storage limits*

Standard storage is the economy sedan that you pick when you really don't care about performance. But you would never bring this car to compete in the NASCAR rally or a Grand Prix. If you want to compete in this arena, your storage needs will only be satisfied through Premium IO. If you compare Figures 5-5 and 5-6, one of the limits that will jump out at you is the megabytes of IO per second. Premium storage provides that as a performance option to consider, whereas Standard storage limits at an IOPs level. As thumb rule, for high performance IO requirements, you should default to Premium storage.

Premium storage supports 64TB of storage for a virtual machine supporting up to 80,000 IOPs and 1600Mbps of throughput at less than one millisecond latency for read operations.

An important point that you need to keep in mind from a cost perspective is the billing difference for Premium versus Standard storage. For a Premium storage account, you will be charged for the allocated size of the disk but for any other type of Storage account, you will only be billed for the storage space used to store the data that is written to the disk regardless of the allocated disk size. So exercise caution while spawning off Premium storage disks to prevent unwarranted shocks in your Azure monthly subscription costs!

Keeping this wisdom in mind, the storage settings showing in Figure 5-7 are for Premium storage configured for Locally Redundant Storage. It is best to use Locally Redundant Storage for Azure disks hosting SQL Server data files. For high availability and disaster recovery, you can configure Availability Groups. The Availability Groups feature is a high-availability and disaster-recovery solution available in SQL Server 2012 and above. The Azure marketplace provides templates for configuring Availability Groups for SQL Server 2012 and above. The example in Figure 5-7 shows how a gallery image based on a template can be used for deploying a fully configured SQL Server instance.

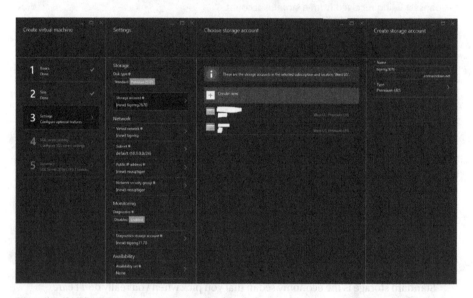

Figure 5-7. *Azure Storage Account settings*

The other settings that you can tweak are the network settings. You can configure the virtual network for your virtual machine, which fences the resources using the same virtual network. This can be used for keeping the SQL Server instances and the application resources for a single business environment within a single subnet. You also have the option of choosing a public or static IP address if there is a strict application dependency on the IP address.

A new concept of Network Security Groups (NSG) was introduced over a year ago and it allows you to create a DMZ-like environment for your virtual machines. Once again network administrators would feel safe and at their data centers when they understand the concept of NSG. A Network Security Group can be applied to a subnet (within a virtual network) or individual virtual machines, which allows you to enable a two-layer protection. The rules within a NSG can be modified and updated independently of the virtual machine, thus allowing the management of access control lists outside the lifecycle of a virtual machine.

A simple use case would be using a NSG to restrict Internet access for virtual machines, as shown in Figure 5-8. One of the great usability features in the NSG configuration is the use of virtual network tags for configuring inbound and outbound rules. Tags are predefined identifiers that represent a category of IP addresses. The Internet tag denotes the public IP address space and will be used to restrict Internet access for the required virtual machines.

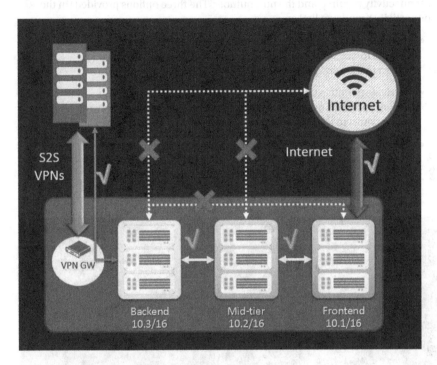

Figure 5-8. *Network security groups*

While configuring the virtual machine, you can configure monitoring (see Figure 5-7). This allows you to enable monitoring for your virtual machine during deployment by attaching a storage account that will host the diagnostic data received from the monitoring endpoints.

Another concept that comes into play is the Availability Set, which helps protect your virtual machines from unplanned and planned maintenance events. If you are deploying a standalone SQL Server instance, an Availability Set is not required. It is recommended that you configure an Availability Set to ensure that maintenance periods do not lead to downtimes for your application production environments hosted on Azure. The availability set is aware of Update/Upgrade and Fault Domains (refer Chapter 2), which ensures that all the machines in your availability set are not taken offline during planned and unplanned maintenance activities. For availability groups, it is best to group all the replica virtual machines in an availability set. *The availability set of a virtual machine can't be changed after it is created.*

SQL Server Settings

If you are using a SQL Server image from the marketplace, these set of configuration options will be offered to configure the SQL Server connectivity, authentication, patching, backup, and storage requirements and key vault configuration.

In Figure 5-9, note that there are two settings available for connectivity, namely the type of connectivity required and the port number. The three options provided (in the SQL Connectivity dropdown list) are:

- Local (inside VM only)—If you do not want connections being made to the SQL Server instance outside the virtual machine, then this is what you should pick.

- Private (within a virtual network)—You should pick this if you want applications and services hosted in the same virtual network to connect to the SQL Server instance.

- Public (Internet)—You should pick this option if you want to connect to the SQL Server instance from another virtual network or from an application like Management Studio running in an on-premises environment.

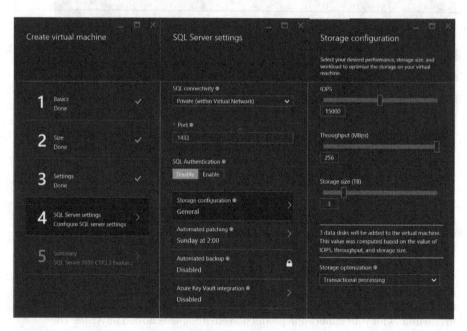

***Figure 5-9.** SQL Server specific configuration settings*

The combination of the SQL Connectivity setting and Network Security Groups provides a powerful tool to lock down access to your SQL Server instance and virtual machine. You can also specify the port that the SQL Server instance will listen on. As a security best practice, it is best to change the default port of 1433 to a different port number to remove a known attack vector. You can also enable SQL Authentication from the same view.

The next configuration option that we are going to discuss is the storage! Storage configuration makes connectivity configuration look like a piece of cake. With the wizard, you have the option of specifying the IOPs, throughput and the storage size required. You also have the option of choosing the type of workload from General, Transactional Processing, and Data Warehousing. Once the inputs are provided, the wizard performs a calculation to determine the best storage configuration. Without this wizard, you would be resigned to attach disks manually to the virtual machine. If you wanted a higher throughput for a single database file and were unable to stripe the data or log file to multiple disks, you would need to configure storage spaces on the Windows Server to help boost IO performance. With this wizard, the right number of disks are attached to the virtual machine during provisioning. If more than one disk is required for the specified settings, the provisioning workflow configures storage spaces (virtual drive) across all disks. Your storage configuration tasks just got really easy!

Before we discuss the additional options available, let us talk about the SQL Server IaaS Agent Extension. This agent is available if you have Azure VM Guest Agent and are deploying SQL Server 2012 or above on Windows Server 2012 or above. This extension allows you to configure automated patching and backup settings for the virtual machine being provisioned. The SQL Automated Patching allows you to configure a maintenance window with a configurable duration for applying updates to your virtual machine without affecting users during peak business hours. The default for this setting is local time 2AM on Sunday for 60 minutes, which can be changed as per your needs. The SQL automated backup configuration allows you to configure as the name suggests automated backups of all your databases hosted on the SQL Server instance to an Azure storage account using the Backup to URL feature. You also have the option of specifying the retention period along with encryption options.

Azure Key Vault provides ease of key management for features like transparent database encryption (TDE), column level encryption and backup encryption. The Azure Key Vault (AKV) service is designed to improve the security and management of encryption keys in a secure and highly available location. The SQL Server Connector enables SQL Server to use these keys from the Azure Key Vault. You can now directly configure the SQL Server instance to use Azure Key Vault while configuring the provisioning inputs for the virtual machine.

Now that you know about all the configuration options, give the deployment wizard a test drive and spawn your optimized SQL Server instance running on an Azure Virtual Machine. Chapter 6 contains more information on deploying hybrid deployments using on-premise instances and also configuring availability groups.

Automating the Automation

Familiarity breeds contempt.

—Aesop

This famous saying should not be taken lightly when you are starting off initially with the ARM cmdlets. Keep the documentation open for reference while writing automation scripts for Azure ARM deployments because muscle memory does take over if you have deployed using PowerShell under the Classic deployment model.

If you manage an enterprise that has a need to provision hundreds of virtual machines on Azure to host SQL Server instances and other applications, you would probably feel the need to automate the steps shown in the earlier section. The need to automate the automation is actually very common among enterprises. Azure allows you to utilize REST APIs, Azure CLI, and PowerShell to automate deployments for virtual machines.

PowerShell always comes to the rescue when there is the need for automation and why should Azure be any different? If you are familiar with the Azure PowerShell cmdlets for the Classic deployment model, most of the ARM PowerShell cmdlets will be easy to get accustomed to as well. The older Azure PowerShell 0.9.x version required you to switch between Azure Resource Manager (ARM) and Azure Service Management (ASM for managing Classic deployment model virtual machines). However, with Azure PowerShell 1.0, you no longer need to switch between ARM and ASM. We will be using Azure PowerShell 1.0 (launched in November 2015) for all the cmdlets that are used in the discussions in this chapter. There are quite a few cmdlets that have a "Rm" substring propped in the middle of the cmdlet that you were used to in the Azure PowerShell 0.9.x version. An example of this is Get-AzureRM, which has an equivalent in the ARM world called Get-AzureRmVM.

Before you begin the Azure PowerShell modules, you need to install them from an administrative PowerShell ISE or command window using the following commands:

```
# Install the Azure Resource Manager modules from the PowerShell Gallery
Install-Module AzureRM
Install-AzureRM
# Import AzureRM modules for the given version manifest in the AzureRM module
Import-AzureRM
```

Keep in mind that the use of an incorrect cmdlet comes to light while the cmdlet is executing. There is no pre-execution check for incorrect use of cmdlets. So if your last cmdlet fails and was part of a single atomic automation block, you will have to repeat the cmdlet execution again. Once too often professionals have been known to use a Classic deployment cmdlet in the ARM world and face the wrath of a PowerShell exception!

Since the previous section covered the portal based deployment as a journey, let us again go through the journey in a scripted manner. Since you will not have the handy mouse click available, you will have to script everything that the UI does under the hood, starting from logging into the correct subscription (see Listing 5-1).

Listing 5-1. PowerShell Code for Logging Into an Azure Subscription

```
## Parameters
$vSubscriptionName = "<subscription name>" # Required if you have multiple
subscriptions
## Import AzureRM
Import-AzureRM

## Log into the Azure and select the correct subscription
Login-AzureRmAccount
Get-AzureRmSubscription -SubscriptionName $vSubscriptionName | Select-
AzureRmSubscription
```

Once you have logged into your Azure account and selected the corrected subscription (if you have access to more than one), you will need to either create the Resource Manager Group, storage account, and other dependent artifacts that you will need to build your virtual machine or use an existing artifact. This chapter assumes that you will create everything from scratch. The first task is to create a resource group and a storage account to host the virtual hard disks for the virtual machine, as shown in Listing 5-2.

Listing 5-2. PowerShell Commands to Create a Resource Group and a Storage Account Associated with the Same Resource Group

```
## Parameters
$vResourceGroupName = "<Resource Group Name>"
$vRegion = "<Region Name>"
$vStorageAccountName = "<Storage Account Name>"
## Create the new resource group
## An Azure resource group is required before you can create any resources
New-AzureRmResourceGroup -Name $vResourceGroupName -Location $vRegion
## Create the storage account and associate it with the Resource Group
New-AzureRmStorageAccount -ResourceGroupName $vResourceGroupName -Location
$vRegion -Name $vStorageAccountName -Type Standard_LRS
## Set the current storage account context to the newly created storage account
Set-AzureRmCurrentStorageAccount -ResourceGroupName $vResourceGroupName
-StorageAccountName $vStorageAccountName
```

Now that you have the housing for the virtual hard disks and a logical container for the resources being created, let's proceed with image selection. This is a bit complicated as the images are updated quite frequently and you need to enumerate based on current list available. Since we used a SQL Server 2016 image earlier in the chapter, we shall endeavor to do the same in this journey. Another selection that you need to zero in on is the virtual image size. Listing 5-3 uses Get-AzureRmVMSize to get a list of all the virtual machine sizes available in the region.

75

Listing 5-3. PowerShell Code to Select the Available Virtual Machine Size and the Latest SQL Server 2016 Image Available in the Gallery

```
$vRegion = "WestUS"
## Get a list of the VMs offered and then make a selection based on the
latest SQL Server 2016 image available
Get-AzureRmVMImageOffer -Location $vRegion -PublisherName
"MicrosoftSQLServer" | Where-Object {$_.Offer -like "*SQL2016*"}
$vImageSelection = Get-AzureRmVMImage -Offer "SQL2016CTP3.3-WS2012R2"
-PublisherName "MicrosoftSQLServer" -Skus "Evaluation" -Location $vRegion
## Get the available virtual machine size and select the appropriate one
Get-AzureRmVMSize -Location $vRegion | Where-Object {$_.MemoryInMB -ge 8192
-and $_.NumberOfCores -ge 4} | ft
$vImageSize = "Standard_DS3"
```

If you are looking to deploy an availability set, you need to use the New-AzureRmAvailabilitySet cmdlet to create a new availability set and add the virtual machine being provisioned (see Listing 5-4). The next task is to create the virtual network. If you are using a standalone instance of SQL Server, you do need an availability set. However, if you are deploying an Availability Group, then an Availability Set is required for completing the configuration. If you deploy Availability Groups using templates available in the gallery, then you will notice that an Availability Set is configured as part of the deployment.

Listing 5-4. Sample Code for Creating an ARM Virtual Network

```
$vNetName = "TigerNet"
## Create the subnet configuration for the vNet
$vSubnet = New-AzureRmVirtualNetworkSubnetConfig -Name "TigerSubnet"
-AddressPrefix "10.0.0.0/24"
## Create the virtual network
$vVNet = New-AzureRmVirtualNetwork -Location $vRegion -Name $vNetName
-ResourceGroupName $vResourceGroupName -Subnet $vSubnet -AddressPrefix
"10.0.0.0/24"
$vNet = Get-AzureRmVirtualNetwork -Name $vNetName  -ResourceGroupName
$vResourceGroupName
$vNetInterface = New-AzureRmNetworkInterface -Name "vNetInterface"
-ResourceGroupName $vResourceGroupName -Location $vNet.Location -SubnetId
$vNet.Subnets[0].Id
```

Now you have all the necessary ingredients to actually create the virtual machine. Listing 5-5 ties together the image size, machine configuration, and the image configuration completed in the earlier sections and asks Azure for a new virtual machine with the provided configuration settings.

Listing 5-5. PowerShell Command to Provision the Virtual Machine

```
$Credential = Get-Credential
$VirtualMachine = New-AzureRmVMConfig -VMName $VMName -VMSize $vImageSize
$VirtualMachine = Set-AzureRmVMOperatingSystem -VM $VirtualMachine -Windows
-ComputerName $ComputerName -Credential $Credential -ProvisionVMAgent
-EnableAutoUpdate
$VirtualMachine = Set-AzureRmVMSourceImage -VM $VirtualMachine
-PublisherName MicrosoftSQLServer -Offer "SQL2016CTP3.3-WS2012R2" -Skus
Evaluation -Version "latest"
$VirtualMachine = Add-AzureRmVMNetworkInterface -VM $VirtualMachine -Id
$Interface.Id
$OSDiskUri = $StorageAccount.PrimaryEndpoints.Blob.ToString() + "vhds/" +
$OSDiskName + ".vhd"
$VirtualMachine = Set-AzureRmVMOSDisk -VM $VirtualMachine -Name $OSDiskName
-VhdUri $OSDiskUri -CreateOption FromImage

## Create the VM in Azure
New-AzureRmVM -ResourceGroupName $ResourceGroupName -Location $Location -VM
$VirtualMachine
```

If you love the Ctrl+C and Ctrl+V feature in Windows, you will love the Get-AzureRmVM PowerShell cmdlet! Get-AzureRmVM fetches the properties of a virtual machine associated with a resource group (see Listing 5-6). It provides a JSON-like output of the model view, which is the user-specified property of the virtual machine like the machine configuration. The output also contains the instance view, which is the instance level status of the virtual machine like the status of the disks attached to the virtual machine. The JSON output can be used to construct virtual machine configurations for future similar deployments. This is highly beneficial when you need to set up test environments that replicate the production environment. Now with Azure PowerShell cmdlets, you can get this done.

Listing 5-6. An Example Output of the Model and Instance View of a Virtual Machine

```
ResourceGroupName        : <...>
Id                       : /subscriptions/<...>/resourceGroups/ninja/
                           providers/Microsoft.Compute/virtualMachines/<...>
Name                     : <...>
Type                     : Microsoft.Azure.Management.Compute.Models.
                           VirtualMachineGetResponse
Location                 : westus
Tags                     : {}
AvailabilitySetReference : null
DiagnosticsProfile       : {
                                "BootDiagnostics": {
                                "Enabled": true,
```

```
                                    "StorageUri":"https://<...>.blob.core.
windows.net/"
                        }
                    }
Extensions                  : [
                        {
                            "AutoUpgradeMinorVersion":false,
                            "ExtensionType":"IaaSDiagnostics",
                            "InstanceView":null,
                            "ProtectedSettings":null,
                            "ProvisioningState":"Succeeded",
                            "Publisher": "Microsoft.Azure.Diagnostics",
                            "Settings": "{\r\n\"xmlCfg\":
\".......\",\r\n  \"storageAccount\": \"<...>\"\r\n}",
                            "TypeHandlerVersion": "1.2",
                            "Id": "/subscriptions/<...>/
resourceGroups/<...>/providers/Microsoft.Compute/virtualMachines/tigerninja/
extensions/Microsoft.Insights.VMDiagnosticsSettings",
                            "Name": "Microsoft.Insights.
                            VMDiagnosticsSettings",
                            "Type": "Microsoft.Compute/virtualMachines/
                            extensions",
                            "Location": "westus",
                            "Tags": {}
                        }
                    ]
HardwareProfile             : {
                            "VirtualMachineSize": "Standard_DS3"
                        }
InstanceView                : null
NetworkProfile              : {
                            "NetworkInterfaces": [
                                {
                                    "Primary": null,
                                    "ReferenceUri": "/subscriptions/<...>/
resourceGroups/ninja/providers/Microsoft.Network/networkInterfaces/<...>"
                                }
                            ]
                        }
OSProfile                   : {
                            "ComputerName": "<...>",
                            "AdminPassword": null,
                            "AdminUsername": "<...>",
                            "CustomData": null,
                            "LinuxConfiguration": null,
                            "Secrets": [],
                            "WindowsConfiguration": {
```

```
                              "AdditionalUnattendContents": [],
                              "EnableAutomaticUpdates": true,
                              "ProvisionVMAgent": true,
                              "TimeZone": null,
                              "WinRMConfiguration": null
                          }
                      }
Plan                  : null
ProvisioningState     : Succeeded
StorageProfile        : {
                          "DataDisks": [
                            {
                              "Lun": 0,
                              "Caching": "ReadOnly",
                              "CreateOption": "Attach",
                              "DiskSizeGB": null,
                              "Name": "datadisk1.vhd",
                              "SourceImage": null,
                              "VirtualHardDisk": {
                                "Uri": "https://<...>.blob.core.windows.
                                net/vhds/datadisk1.vhd"
                              }
                            },
                            {
                              "Lun": 1,
                              "Caching": "ReadOnly",
                              "CreateOption": "Attach",
                              "DiskSizeGB": null,
                              "Name": "datadisk2.vhd",
                              "SourceImage": null,
                              "VirtualHardDisk": {
                                "Uri": "https://<...>.blob.core.windows.
                                net/vhds/datadisk2.vhd"
                              }
                            },
                            {
                              "Lun": 2,
                              "Caching": "None",
                              "CreateOption": "Attach",
                              "DiskSizeGB": null,
                              "Name": "logdisk.vhd",
                              "SourceImage": null,
                              "VirtualHardDisk": {
                                "Uri": "https://<...>.blob.core.windows.
                                net/vhds/logdisk.vhd"
                              }
                            },
```

```
                                    {
                                      "Lun": 3,
                                      "Caching": "ReadOnly",
                                      "CreateOption": "Empty",
                                      "DiskSizeGB": 128,
                                      "Name": "<...>-20151017-015414",
                                      "SourceImage": null,
                                      "VirtualHardDisk": {
                                        "Uri": "https://<...>.blob.core.windows.
                                        net/vhds/<...>-20151017-015414.vhd"
                                      }
                                    }
                                  ],
                                  "ImageReference": {
                                    "Offer": "WindowsServer",
                                    "Publisher": "MicrosoftWindowsServer",
                                    "Sku": "2012-R2-Datacenter",
                                    "Version": "latest"
                                  },
                                  "OSDisk": {
                                    "OperatingSystemType": "Windows",
                                    "Caching": "ReadWrite",
                                    "CreateOption": "FromImage",
                                    "DiskSizeGB": null,
                                    "Name": "tigerninja",
                                    "SourceImage": null,
                                    "VirtualHardDisk": {
                                      "Uri": "https://<...>.blob.core.windows.
                                      net/vhds/<...>.vhd"
                                    }
                                  }
                                }
DataDiskNames            : {datadisk1.vhd, datadisk2.vhd, logdisk.vhd,
                           tigerninja-20151017-015414...}
NetworkInterfaceIDs      : {/subscriptions/<...>/resourceGroups/ninja/
                           providers/Microsoft.Network/networkInter
                           faces/<...>}
```

Post Deployment

Once the virtual machine deployment is complete, you will notice that there is a pretty useful diagnostics view of the alerts and resource usage. This can be further customized to your liking by adding tiles and groups and resizing the tiles (see Figure 5-10) as per your whims and fancies or business requirements. One of the most useful aspects of these tiles is that they can be pinned to your dashboard. So if you have a critical metric that you want to monitor, you could have it pinned on your dashboard that's visible to you as soon as you log into the Azure web portal.

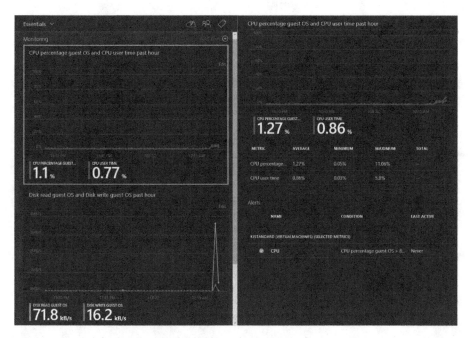

Figure 5-10. *Azure Virtual Machine diagnostics view*

If you find that a particular performance metric is very important for your business, then you can add an alert for the performance monitor data based on a threshold. As you can see in Figure 5-10, there is a CPU usage alert defined for the guest OS when it's greater than 80. When the alert is raised, you can automatically send an e-mail to administrators of the virtual machine. If you need the alert notification sent to a specific group without your company, then you can add other recipients as well.

If you think e-mail is old school, you can take this a step further by configuring web hooks for your alerts. Azure provides the capability to use HTTP or HTTPS endpoints to send JSON payloads using POST methods. If you already have tools that process incoming web requests to create paging and service requests, your job becomes even simpler! Your support staff can seamlessly work on service requests without having to worry about setting up additional diagnostics and alerts for these environments. If you were thinking about reducing the learning curve and maximizing the efficiency curve, this is definitely a functionality that deserves a thumbs up for hitting the nail on the head!

If you feel the need to add metrics that need to be monitored, this can be done using the Diagnostics option available under the Monitoring group in the All Settings blade view. Azure does not add any alerts by default, so you would need to add the alerts pertinent to your business under the Alerts option available under the same Monitoring group.

With the advent of Azure Automation, you can convert a number of the PowerShell scripts into automation runbooks, which can be reused by multiple users having access to the Azure Automation account. You can use Azure Automation runbooks to run post install custom configuration like setting up user databases or even additional configuration for your Analysis Services, Reporting Services, and Integration Services.

Azure Resource Explorer

If you want to get the JSON representation of any of the ARM resources that you have deployed or even others have deployed in your subscription (provided you have permissions), then head over to Azure Resource Explorer (`resources.azure.com`). This is another Ctrl+C and Ctrl+V experience of sorts, albeit a bit new if you are not too familiar with the jargon of GET and PUT! You can use the Web UI to browse the resources in your subscription.

Before we digress too much, the Azure Resource Explorer provides a way to inspect your existing deployments and create templates out of them. There are a bunch of templates available on GitHub under Azure-QuickStart-Templates. If you are feeling adventurous, then you can create an Azure Resource Manager template from scratch using Visual Studio 2015. However, be forewarned that even the most seasoned professionals have been known to tear their virtual hair out for overlooking obvious omissions during debugging errors while creating templates from scratch. One of the most innocuous examples of such frustration was the inability to figure out the non-usage of a strong password during a virtual machine deployment.

The right pane shown in Figure 5-11 provides the GET and PUT options for your resource. You also get the documentation for your resource methods and the PowerShell equivalent commands for creating your resource when you click on the Documentation and PowerShell tabs respectively. An Azure template has the following components:

- Schema provides the location of the JSON schema file, which describes the version of the template language. In today's fast-changing world, this is very important.

- Content Version specifies the version of the template to be used.

- Parameters are values that can be customized for each deployment.

- Variables are used as JSON fragments in the template to simplify the template language expressions.

- Resources are the types of services that are deployed or updated, like virtual machines, storage accounts, etc.

The following PowerShell code from Azure Resource Explorer UI is used to get a virtual machine's instance and model view:

```
$vRM = Get-AzureRmResource -ResourceGroupName <resource group name>
-ResourceType Microsoft.Compute/virtualMachines -ResourceName <resource
name> -ApiVersion 2015-06-15
## Additional command to get the list of data disks attached to the virtual
machine
$vRM.Properties.StorageProfile.DataDisks
```

If you click on the Actions (POST, DELETE) tab as showing Figure 5-11, you will be able to perform a number of actions against your resource like shutting down, restarting, and starting your virtual machine and even deleting the resource. The UI also provides the equivalent action methods like POST and DELETE. Actions are possible only if you are in Read/Write mode. Once you have a template file available, you can use the New-AzureRmResourceGroupDeployment cmdlet to perform a deployment using the JSON template. This cmdlet provides an option to specify a list of parameters using the -TemplateParameterFile switch.

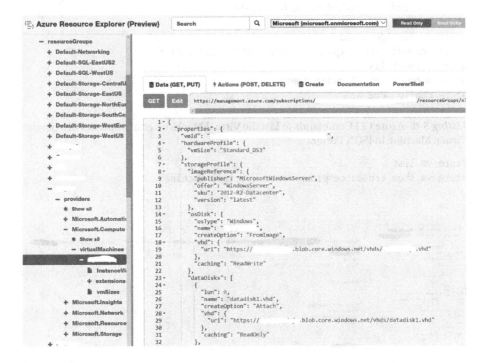

Figure 5-11. *Azure Resource Manager portal*

Azure CLI

If you are *an* automation fan, then the Azure Command Line Interface (CLI) is probably the next download that you will be performing! Microsoft Azure Xplat-CLI for Windows, Mac and Linux is a project that provides a cross-platform command line interface for developers and IT administrators to develop, deploy, and manage Microsoft Azure applications. The CLI version referenced in this chapter is 0.9.15 (node: 4.2.4). You will need to have node.js installed on your machine to operate Azure CLI.

Before you can start using the CLI commands, you will need to configure your settings and log into your subscription. Listings 5-7 and 5-8 log into Azure, which requires you to provide your authentication details and a code on the Azure web site. Then you can download your management settings file, which is imported into your account. Then the accounts (if more than one) are listed and the desired subscription is set as the default. Finally, the operation mode is set to ARM to view the ARM resources associated with the subscription. The version of CLI being referenced operates under the Classic deployment model by default.

Listing 5-7. Commands to Log Into Azure and Use the Desired Subscription for ARM Operations

```
azure login

To sign in, use a web browser to open the page http://aka.ms/devicelogin.
Enter the code XXXXXXXXX to authenticate.

azure account download
azure account import <path to your .publishsettings file>
azure account list
azure account set <Account Name>
azure config mode arm
```

Listing 5-8. Azure CLI Commands to List the Virtual Machines and Properties of a Single Virtual Machine in JSON Format

```
azure vm list
azure vm show <resource group name> <virtual machine>
```

Figure 5-12. *Azure CLI output snippet for the azure vm show command*

Summary

In this chapter, you learned how SQL Server instances can be deployed on Azure Virtual Machines using the wizard and through automation. We also discussed a number of considerations that will impact performance and the cost of your virtual machines.

CHAPTER 6

■ ■ ■

SQL Hybrid Solutions

With all the business dynamics available in today's IT industry, there is a huge paradigm shift. You need to constantly innovate and grow your business by reducing the Total Cost of Ownership (TCO) and maximizing the return on investment. Microsoft Azure provides you with a perfect platform to accomplish this by integrating the public cloud resources and private cloud resources together. The classic case of hybrid cloud usage is to store your sensitive data within your on-premises data center and connect to the public cloud where other data resides.

The hybrid cloud provides a bridge between your on-premises data center and your public cloud. Microsoft's approach to the cloud is quite unique as there is consistency across the cloud in terms of the servers that are being used in the data centers. Any customer can optimize resources depending on their needs and can store critical and secure data in their on-premise data centers and leverage the storage cost by offloading the work to the cloud, thereby scaling up without actually impacting cost.

SQL Server integrates quite well with cloud services from Azure, providing end-to-end experiences, using the same interface as T-SQL or PowerShell that you are comfortable with. Hybrid environments are environments where the resources come from the cloud and the resources come from on-premises sites. The resources are physical machines, VMs, storage (SAN, Cloud Storage), DC (for ADs , logins policies, etc.), and databases. So you can think of couple ways to run your hybrid environment. Say you can have a SQL Server that runs on-premises and that uses cloud resources. You could have your SQL Server in the cloud using an on-premise resource. When we think of going hybrid with SQL Server running within our on-premises environment talking to the cloud, we use two resources: Azure storage and Azure Virtual Machines.

Microsoft Azure enables you to store a huge amount of data with minimal risk due to the multiple replicas that the data gets written to. To add to this, there is automated disk healing that runs a checksum to ensure that the data is logically consistent.

If the checksum doesn't match, we automatically take the disk out and then make another copy on the fly. This means having three copies of the data at any point in time. Cost is also low, which is one reason why customers are moving to Azure. Another important resource is virtual machines, which are available in Azure. These VMs are highly available and offer automatic VM healing with a plethora of sizes you can choose from and are a great cost-saver.

Figure 6-1 shows different scenarios we can leverage in the cloud infrastructure to save cost. For example, we can store backups to Azure storage, store SQL Server files in Azure storage, and use the AlwaysOn technology to extend the on-premises infrastructure

© Pranab Mazumdar, Sourabh Agarwal, Amit Banerjee 2016

P. Mazumdar et al., *Pro SQL Server on Microsoft Azure*, DOI 10.1007/978-1-4842-2083-2_6

and have a secondary site configured in the cloud. We will look at these in detail later in this chapter.

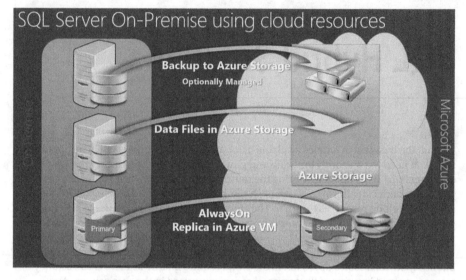

Figure 6-1. *On-premises integration using Azure Storage*

Hybrid Model Snapshot

The hybrid model provides the following advantages:

- Your business decision become agile and you can quickly make decisions about making resources available with this model.

- You don't end up wasting time getting the machines ready (hardware/software); instead you can focus on more productive business logic or possibly serve the customer's need.

- You can now leverage the Microsoft Azure ecosystem of applications and build a highly scalable application.

However, when you go with this hybrid infrastructure, there are few factors to consider:

- You may have to think over maintaining the hybrid infrastructure, as there are additional components to it like a firewall, virtual networks, routing devices, etc.

- Managing and accessing the resources involves different sorts of applications, thus classic consolidation could be a challenge.

- Before moving to the cloud, you should evaluate the complexity, perform risk assessment, and do a benchmark study on the feasibility.

The applications, tools, and services running on either side are not always interoperable. There are several applications that cannot quite cross these boundaries and thus it is important for you to evaluate the pros and the cons.

Backups to Azure Storage

With SQL Server 2014 BackuptoUrl was enhanced and can now perform the backups and store the files directly on to the Microsoft Azure Storage. This way, you can store database backups from on-premises, Azure VMs to store backups in Azure storage, and leverage the features of Azure storage (built-in redundancy and replication of data for designing your DR strategy massively scalable). This is accomplished through a REST API instead of HTTP to interact with the Azure storage. Basically, all you need are the following:

- Microsoft Azure account

- Azure storage account

- Container inside the storage account

- SAS key

You can read more about the SAS keys here: https://azure.microsoft.com/en-us/ documentation/articles/storage-dotnet-shared-access-signature-part-1/.

Figure 6-2 depicts the backup and restore feature, where the backups are stored within Azure storage. You can easily perform a restore from there.

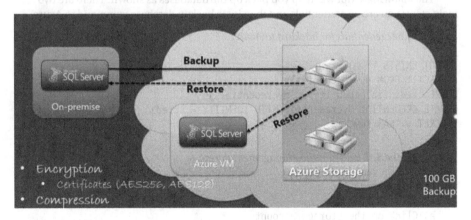

Figure 6-2. *Backup in Azure storage*

With SQL 2014, we used the Backup2Url or the Smart Backup to accomplish the backups. The backups used to be in page blobs. Page blobs are optimized for random reads and writes. With SQL 2016, this feature is enhanced and will be taken to the next level where you can backup to block blobs, which is supposed to be more economical for the customers. Apart from this, there are few advantages of this architecture. The Backup/Restore can be done to/from stripped sets, which was not possible with page blobs or Backup2Url. There have been some enhancements made with backup to blobs, which will further enhance the restore experience.

Figure 6-3 shows how you can leverage the hybrid environment and store the backups (Full Transactional here) of the databases in Azure storage, thereby helping business reduce total cost.

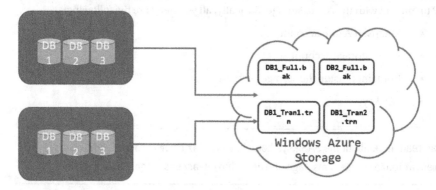

Figure 6-3. *Database backup files in Microsoft Azure Storage*

The following script will help you back up the databases as shown. There are two main steps: you create credentials and then issue backup database command to Azure.

Step 1: Create credentials for backups to Azure

```
IF NOT EXISTS
(SELECT * FROM sys.credentials
WHERE credential_identity = 'mycredential')
CREATE CREDENTIAL mycredential WITH IDENTITY = 'cred1'
,SECRET = 'SAS Key' ;
```

You can get the SAS key from the Management portal:

```
Old/Classic Portal :-

    a) Click on the storage account
    b) Click on the Manage Access keys.
    c) You will find the primary and the secondary keys to access the
       storage account.
N.B:- Once you click on the storage account, click the "Containers" Tab, you
can add a container and call it as testcontainer using the Add option here.
```

New Portal:-
    a) Create the Storage account
    b) Click on the storage account
    c) Under Settings , Click Access keys
    d) You will find the primary and secondary keys under the storage
       account name.

In the new portal, click on the storage account and then on the blob services, as shown in Figure 6-4. You'll see different storage services.

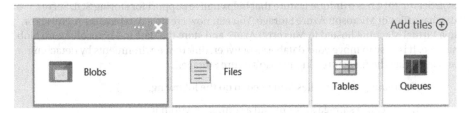

Figure 6-4. *Storage services as shown in the new portal*

You can add the container using the + sign shown in Figure 6-5. As you click on the Blobs service (see Figure 6-4), you will get the different options, as shown in Figure 6-5.

Figure 6-5. *Adding a container to the new portal*

Now name the container testcontainer and choose the appropriate access type, as follows.

Step 2: Issue a backup database command for backups to Azure

```
BACKUP DATABASE DB1
TO URL ='https://storageaccountname.blob.core.windows.net/testcontainer/
DB1_Full.bak'
WITH CREDENTIAL = 'cred1',
COMPRESSION,
STATS = 5;
GO
BACKUP DATABASE DB2
TO URL ='https://storageaccountname.blob.core.windows.net/testcontainer/
DB2_Full.bak'
```

```
WITH CREDENTIAL = 'cred1',
COMPRESSION,
STATS = 5;
GO
```

Similarly, you can also back up the log files to the container in the Azure storage account.

SQL Server Files in Microsoft Azure Storage

SQL Server 2014 has a unique feature that helps native support for storing SQL Server database files in Microsoft Azure Storage. You can now create a database on-premises or in a Virtual Machine hosted in Microsoft Azure and store the data in Microsoft Azure blob storage. It is easy to move your databases between different environments by detaching and attaching the files stored in Microsoft Azure Storage.

While creating the data files, you need to do the following:

1. Create a storage account and a container within it.

2. Create a SQL Server credential that has the policy of the container.

3. Access the container using Shared Access Signature.

While using the native feature of storing the files in the Microsoft Azure Storage, you need to:

1. Create a policy on the container and generate the SAS key. To get the SAS key, download Microsoft Storage Explorer from https://azurestorageexplorer.codeplex.com/.

2. For each container you need a credential and its name should match the containers path.

Figure 6-6 shows that you can have your databases residing on-premises or on an Azure Virtual Machine in Microsoft Azure.

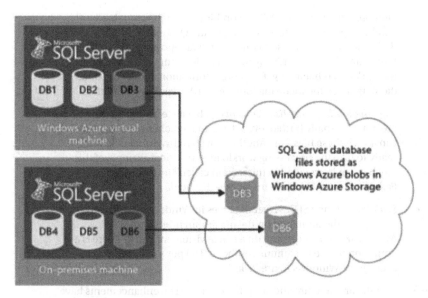

Figure 6-6. *Data files as stored in a Microsoft Azure Storage account*

As you can see, we have DB3 created in an Azure Virtual Machine with its files residing on the Azure storage. On the other hand, DB6 is residing on the on-premises environment and has the files stored in the Azure storage. The advantages of using SQL Server data files on Windows Azure blob storage service are as follows:

- *Portability*. It's easy to detach a database from a Windows Azure Virtual Machine (IaaS) and attach the database to a different virtual machine in the cloud; this feature might be also suitable to implement an efficient disaster recovery mechanism, because everything is directly accessible in Windows Azure blob storage. To migrate or move databases, use a single CREATE DATABASE Transact-SQL query that refers to the blob locations, with no restrictions on storage account and compute resource location. You can also use rolling upgrade scenarios if extended downtime for operating system and/or SQL Server maintenance is required.

- *Database virtualization.* When combined with the contained database feature in SQL Server 2012 and SQL Server 2014, a database can now be a self-contained data repository for each tenant and then dynamically moved to different virtual machines for workload rebalancing. For more information about contained databases, see the following topic in SQL Server Books Online:

- *High availability and disaster recovery.* Because all database files are now externally hosted, even if a virtual machine crashes, you can attach these files from another hot standby virtual machine, ready to take the processing workload. A practical example of this mechanism is provided in the section called "Implementing a Failover Cluster Mechanism" later in this book.

- *Scalability.* Using SQL Server data files in Windows Azure, you can bypass the limitation on the maximum number of Windows Azure disks you can mount on a single virtual machine. There is a limitation on the maximum number of I/O per second (IOPS) for each single Windows Azure disk.

Let's look at the architecture and simplify this a bit. The enhancements have been made within the SQL Server engine layer itself. There are three layers where the integration has been done; Figure 6-7 will simplify this idea a bit.

- *Manager layer.* This includes a new component called XFCB Credential Manager, which manages the security credentials necessary to access the Windows Azure blob containers and provides the necessary security interface. Secrets are maintained encrypted and secured in the SQL Server built-in security repository in the master system database.

- *File Control layer.* Contains a new object called XFCB, which is the Windows Azure extension to the file control block (FCB) used to manage IO against each single SQL Server data or log file on the NTFS file system; it implements all the APIs that are required for IO against Windows Azure blob storage.

- *Storage layer.* At the Storage layer, the SQL Server I/O Manager is now able to natively generate REST API calls to Windows Azure blob storage with minimal overhead and great efficiency; in addition, this component can generate information about performance counters and extended events (xEvents).

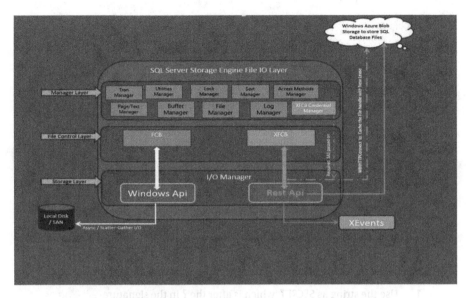

Figure 6-7. *SQL Server Storage Engineer File IO*

Here is an example of creating a sample database using this concept:

```
-- Creating Databases with files in Windows Azure Storage
-- Step 1: Create a credential
CREATE CREDENTIAL [https://storageaccountName.blob.core.windows.net/
testcontainer]
WITH IDENTITY='SHARED ACCESS SIGNATURE',
SECRET = 'SECRET KEY'
```

This secret key is generated using the Azure Storage Explorer.

1. Choose testcontainer and click on the security button on the toolbar.

2. Click the Shared Access Signatures tab.

3. Click the Generate Signature button to generate the SAS signature (see Figure 6-8).

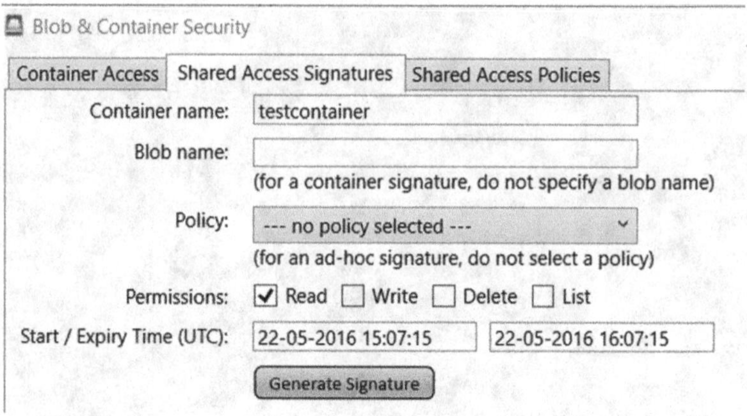

Blob & Container Security

Container Access	Shared Access Signatures	Shared Access Policies

Container name: `testcontainer`

Blob name: _____

(for a container signature, do not specify a blob name)

Policy: `--- no policy selected ---` ▾

(for an ad-hoc signature, do not select a policy)

Permissions: ☑ Read ☐ Write ☐ Delete ☐ List

Start / Expiry Time (UTC): `22-05-2016 15:07:15`   `22-05-2016 16:07:15`

Generate Signature

Figure 6-8. Blob & Container Security Dialog: Storage Explorer

Once you get the string using the data in Figure 6-8, follow these steps.

1. Use the string as SECRET, which is after the ? in the signature string.

2. Create a database with data and log files in an Windows Azure container as follows:

```
CREATE DATABASE FirstHybridDB
ON
( NAME = FirstHybridDB_dat,
    FILENAME = 'https://storageaccountname.blob.core.windows.net/
    testcontainer/FirstHybridDB.mdf' )
 LOG ON
( NAME = FirstHybridDB_log,
    FILENAME =  'https://storageaccountname.blob.core.windows.net/
    testcontainer/FirstHybridDB_Log.ldf')
```

Smart Backup

Smart Backup is one of the new features of SQL Server 2014 that uses the Azure infrastructure for taking intelligent backups. Following are a few of the key differences with traditional backups:

- Backup is based on intelligence rather than on schedule

- Completely managed by SQL Server

- Backup retention is automatically managed

- Backup retrieval is more reliable

Smart Backup can be configured at the instance level or at the DB level. The only input parameter required is the retention period, which ranges from 1 to 30 days. When Smart Backup is enabled at instance level, existing databases need to be added manually; however new databases will automatically be added to the schedule. Backups can be stored in encrypted or unencrypted form. To enhance security, keys can be regenerated at regular intervals. The following script needs to be run to enable this feature:

```
-- Enable Smart Backups

EXEC smart_admin.sp_set_db_backup
               @database_name='TestDB',
               @retention_days=30,
               @credential_name='cred1',
               @encryption_algorithm='NO_ENCRYPTION',
               @enable_backup=1
GO
```

If you want backups that are created using the smart backup feature to be encrypted, you need to create the key, certificate, and the credentials. You could have the key rotated at regular intervals for security purposes; this can be done by using the secondary key and regenerating it (see Listing 6-1).

Listing 6-1. Creating the Key for Smart Backup Encryption

```
Use master;
Go
--Create a master key
Create master key encryption by password='Password@123'
Go
--Create a certificate
Create certificate mycert1 With subject ='MySmartBackup'

If exist (select * from sys.credentials where name = 'cred1')

Drop credential cred1
--Create a Credential
Create credential cred1
With identity ='StorageAccountName',
Secret = 'SAS KEY'

--Smart backup enabled at Instance level.
Use msdb;
GO
EXEC smart_admin.sp_set_instance_backup
               --@database_name='TestDB'
                @retention_days=30
               ,@credential_name='cred1'
               ,@encryption_algorithm ='AES_128'
```

```
              ,@encryptor_type= 'Certificate'
              ,@encryptor_name='mycert1'
              ,@enable_backup=1;
GO

-- Smart backup enabled at DB level.
Use msdb;
GO
EXEC smart_admin.sp_set_db_backup
              @database_name='TestDB'
              ,@retention_days=30
              ,@credential_name='mycred1'
              ,@encryption_algorithm ='AES_128'
              ,@encryptor_type= 'Certificate'
              ,@encryptor_name='Mycert1'
              ,@enable_backup=1;
GO

--View managed backup configuration at the instance level

Select * from msdb.smart_admin.fn_backup_instance_config ()

--View configuration details

Select * from msdb.smart_admin.fn_backup_db_config ('')
```

For ad hoc backups, use the following, but note that it could break the chain and a fresh full backup would need to be triggered:

```
--On Demand backup to the cloud

exec msdb.smart_admin.sp_backup_on_demand 'TestDB','log'

exec msdb.smart_admin.sp_backup_on_demand 'TestDB','database'
```

The following provides more information on how to create backups for a database with SQL Server managed backups to Windows Azure.

```
https://msdn.microsoft.com/en-IN/library/dn451012.aspx
```

AlwaysOn Configuration on Azure VMs

AlwaysOn has evolved over the years. Many of our customers can't afford a DR site. They can be costly in terms of purchasing the hardware, maintenance can be an overhead, and you need to have an operations team to run the site. So it adds to your total cost. For such customers, we wanted to provide a solution for disaster recovery and therefore, starting in 2012, we added replica in Microsoft Azure (VMs). This is an IaaS offering where you can have SQL server running on virtual machines. As it stands today, we have quite a few customers who run their reporting workload on the Azure and take backups from there and can use it as a DR site. This way, they offload the backups and don't touch the primary server. There are a few points to check before making such a setup:

- The latency shouldn't be so much that the secondary can't catch up and ends up lagging far behind.

- Confirm that the data that's stored in the secondary replica on a different data center complies with the data protection and security norms.

You can have your main data center on-premises and add your secondary replica on Azure. The requirements needed for this setup are discussed shortly.

In 2014, we introduced a new wizard where you can add the replica in the cloud, end-to-end. Suppose you needed to configure an AlwaysOn Availability Group, and you know that you need machines. You would need to install Windows Failover Cluster, and then you would need to enable AlwaysOn, take a backup and restore it, and then post it to start synchronization. The environment is then validated using this new wizard.

This wizard also has built-in logic, whereby if there is a failure it will retry automatically. It has timeouts set as well.

Today, its easy to extend the Availability Group to Azure VM; it is cheap compared to keeping it on-premises. In this case, you need to pay for VM, storage, and the traffic going out. You get free ingress traffic and with no DR site cost in terms of hardware, so it works quite well for a DR site. You have your secondary replica in a different site, so during DR you manually failover to the secondary replica. You can thus offload your work to the primary site, i.e., reporting and BI to the readable secondary on Azure. You can take backups as well. The only thing that you need to do is configure site-to-site VPN tunnel between on-premises and Azure. After you do this, you can extend your AlwaysOn configuration.

The following are the requirements for extending your on-premises data center with AlwaysOn AG:

- A valid subscription

- An existing AlwaysOn Availability group within your on-premises network

- Connectivity between your on-premises network and the Azure Virtual Network using a VPN device. You can read more here: https://azure.microsoft.com/en-in/documentation/articles/vpn-gateway-site-to-site-create/

Once this is done, you can use the Add Azure Replica wizard, which will help you extend your existing AG by adding another replica to the Microsoft Azure as follows:

1. From SQL Server Management Studio, go to AlwaysOn Availability Group and then Availability Groups to provide the name of the Availability Group.

2. Right-click on the availability replicas and then click on Add Replica.

3. The wizard shown in Figure 6-9 appears.

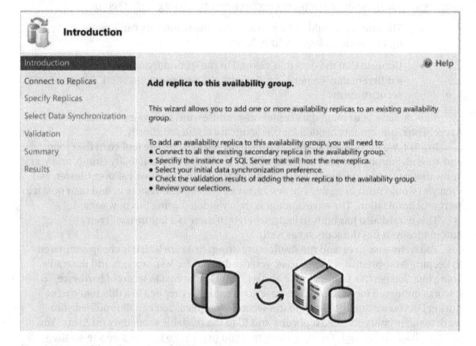

Figure 6-9. Add replica wizard GUI

4. Connect to your existing replicas by using the Connect or Connect All button.

5. On the next screen, you will be presented with Figure 6-10.

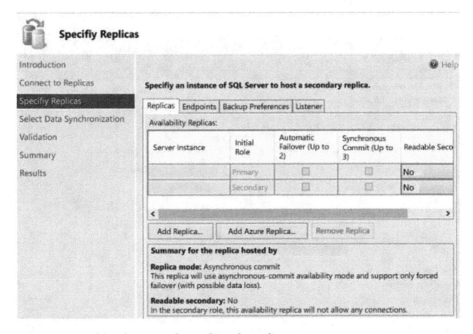

Figure 6-10. *Add replica wizard: specifying the replicas*

6. From this screen, click on the Replica tab and then click the Add Azure Replica button.

7. Now download the certificate or use an existing one (see Figure 6-11).

Figure 6-11. *Certificate download screen*

You should populate these fields, as this information is crucial and will be used in creating the new Azure replica.

---

8. After this, you will be back to the Add Azure Replica page, where you need to validate/provide the information in the other tabs, such as backup preference and endpoints.

9. Select the data synchronization type as per your business requirement. You can read more here: `https://msdn.microsoft.com/library/hh231021.aspx`.

Once you're done, you can review the validation page, correct the issues identified, and re-run the wizard. Once you're done, you will have a replica in Microsoft Azure. You should create a listener for the clients to connect to the replicas. The listener redirects the incoming requests to the primary or the secondary replica. Refer to the Azure documentation or the links provided next to explore this concept and its implementation more.

Summary

In today's world, managing resources more effectively by utilizing the power of Microsoft Azure platform is critical for your business. You can be more agile and manage your resources more efficiently. You can extend your on-premises data center with the Microsoft public cloud and leverage the so-called hybrid model, which gives you a chance to leverage the best of both environments. With this model you can easily move your business and workloads from different data centers. Today, your application is capable of taking advantage of the public cloud using Microsoft Azure storage, storing backups, and securely storing your data, all the while seamlessly working on your existing private cloud environment.

Additional References

Use the Add Azure Replica wizard

```
https://msdn.microsoft.com/en-in/library/dn463980.aspx
```

Use the Add Replica to Availability Group wizard

```
https://msdn.microsoft.com/en-us/library/hh213239.aspx
```

Protect SQL Server with SQL Server disaster recovery and Azure site recovery

```
https://azure.microsoft.com/en-in/documentation/articles/site-recovery-sql/
```

CHAPTER 7

■ ■ ■

All About Performance

In the previous chapters, we talked about deploying the SQL Server instance in various combinations on an Azure Virtual Machine (Azure VM). We had touched upon a few of the best practices that would allow you to get an optimal configuration from the get-go. However, there might be scenarios where you would need to run health checks on your environment to ensure that is configured for optimal performance. Additionally, you might feel the need to run an impromptu health check while troubleshooting performance problems for a SQL Server instance running on an Azure VM. In this chapter, we will discuss the similarities and the differences that you would need to keep in mind while optimizing for performance for a SQL Server environment hosted on an Azure VM.

If you needed to understand the value of following best practices and recommendations on Azure, then it would be best explained with the example of post-sales servicing for an ultra-luxury car and an economy sedan or SUV. If you buy an ultra-luxury car, then the trips to the service center are mighty heavy on the pocket, cost a small fortune, and over the years can fund an economy sedan. While the ultra-luxury car does have the snob value, feels luxurious, and is eye catching, it does nothing from a common sense economics standpoint. So if you want your post sales (i.e. post deployment in Azure) to be economical, efficient, and high performing, then you need to pay extra care to the best practices. Simple things like the location of your application and database services can be your best friend and worst enemy.

One of the most common pitfalls in Azure is that the driving principles of choosing your compute and storage remain the same. However, the onus on choosing the configuration is now on the software application management team rather than the hardware procurement team. An important point to keep in mind as well is *multi-tenancy*. In a multi-tenant world, everyone has the same SLAs. Physically accessing the hardware is not possible and you are so far abstracted from the actual backend that system provides the functionality as a service. The very concept of "as a service" in today's world works on the principle of commoditizing hardware, abstracting the internals, and providing the components the customer needs.

© Pranab Mazumdar, Sourabh Agarwal, Amit Banerjee 2016
P. Mazumdar et al., *Pro SQL Server on Microsoft Azure*, DOI 10.1007/978-1-4842-2083-2_7

■ **Note** All the PowerShell script examples are available in the following project on GitHub repository: **github.com/amitmsft/SqlOnAzureVM**. The PowerShell samples in this chapter assume that the virtual machine is deployed under the Resource Manager model and you already have Azure Resource Manager cmdlets installed on the server where these PowerShell scripts are being executed. The PowerShell script files can be downloaded from the GitHub repository mentioned earlier in this chapter or can be executed by saving the snippets as `.ps1` files. The examples shown in this chapter assume that the scripts will be executed on a machine that has the SQL Server instance being assessed.

Understanding the Virtual Machine Performance

Virtualization has become a ubiquitous term with IT environments today. There was a wave in the industry to gravitate toward virtualization and now there is a wave to gravitate toward the cloud. Since Infrastructure as a Service (IaaS) closely resembles what a virtual environment would like in a private data center, there are similarities that can be pitfalls and there are differences that you should be aware of. In Chapter 2, we talked about the Azure architecture, which showed that there are a large number of components that bind the compute and storage components into a virtual machine. This environment may look like your on-premises virtual machine but it's vastly different from it under the hood. In this section, we will talk about the best practices that are required to run your SQL Server instance optimally without incurring any performance penalties due to misconfigurations or failure to follow best practices. Let's first take a look at compute and storage performance aspects.

Compute

It is recommended (based on testing done by Microsoft) that you use a DS3 machine for the Enterprise Edition and DS2 machine for the Standard Edition. One of the main reasons for this is due to the availability of the local SSD, which can be utilized for tempdb and also because Premium IO disks can be attached to these machines. Azure Storage and its different tiers were highlighted in Chapter 3. If such a check had to be automated against multiple machines, then this could be done using the weapon of choice of an automation ninja; i.e., PowerShell. Listing 7-1 shows how to check if you are running a DS- or G-series virtual machine hosting a SQL Server instance.

Listing 7-1. PowerShell Code to Check if an Azure VM Hosting a SQL Server Instance Is Running the Recommended Tier

```
$RGName = "<Resource Group Name>"
$VMName = "<ARM deployed virtual machine name>"
# Get the details of the virtual machine
$VM = Get-AzureRmVM -ResourceGroupName $RGName -Name $VMName
# Check if the recommended machine size is being followed
if ($VM.HardwareProfile.VirtualMachineSize -like ("*_DS*") -or $VM.
HardwareProfile.VirtualMachineSize -like "*_G*")
{
    Write-Host "[INFO] Virtual machine size: " $VM.HardwareProfile.
    VirtualMachineSize -ForegroundColor Green
}
else
{
    Write-Host "[WARN] Virtual machine size: " $VM.HardwareProfile.
    VirtualMachineSize -ForegroundColor Yellow
    Write-Host "It is recommended to use DS2 or higher machines for SQL
    Server Standard Edition" -ForegroundColor Yellow
    Write-Host "It is recommended to use DS3 or higher machines for SQL
    Server Enterprise Edition" -ForegroundColor Yellow
}
```

Another consideration with respect to choosing a larger virtual machine is the network bandwidth. The larger the machine, the more network bandwidth you have. It is important to note that network communications generated by accessing data disks and the operating system disk attached to the virtual machine are not considered part of the bandwidth limits.

Network

One of the fundamental differences in Azure related to networking is that the latency can be higher as compared to your traditional on-premises environment due to multiple layers that are introduced, such as load balancers, firewalls, virtualization, etc. *One of the golden rules of optimizing network performance for your applications talking to SQL Server is to reduce the number of network round trips.* If you are unable to do so, it is recommended that you consolidate the application layers into a single virtual machine of an appropriate tier. This ensures that the network calls do not have to leave the virtual machine.

If you have applications or systems that make the upward journey to the cloud from your on-premises environment, it's best to determine the network profile of the application calls to the database along with the chattiness quotient. In scenarios where none of the changes required to control the chattiness and network round trips can be changed as desired, you might consider using Azure ExpressRoute, which can create private connections between Azure data centers and on-premises infrastructure or in a co-location environment. You can reach bandwidths as high as 10Gbps depending on the tier that you choose and your geographical location.

■ **Note** Microsoft uses ExpressRoute configurations for hybrid deployments of internal applications and has seen high levels of performance improvement in these environments as opposed to when ExpressRoute was not used.

Ctrl+C and Ctrl+V are truly awesome features adored by IT professionals across the world and this at times can become the bane of your performance. Moving any sort of data to and from your virtual machine and an on-premises environment using copy and paste functionality or any other means counts toward your bandwidth consumption. So it is time to cringe when you see that developer running a SELECT * query on a table with a million rows against a Management Studio running on the on-premises machine while connecting to a SQL Server instance hosted on an Azure VM! It is always advisable to set up a client workstation(s) in Azure that the developer(s) can use for development/testing efforts. If there is a need to move data in and out of the Azure region or on-premises, it's better to compress the data before moving it for performance and cost reasons.

Storage

The next aspect of performance is the configuration of the storage layout. *The Azure Storage account and compute for your virtual machine should be in the same data center to reduce transfer delays.* If you fail to do this, performance is negatively impacted exponentially. This is akin to having your bed in one room and the mattress in the other. The functionality of the mattress might be served but the true value of both the components put together will never be realized unless they are bundled together!

It is recommended to use SQL Server features for high availability and disaster recovery for the instance and databases hosted on the instance, as consistent write order across multiple disks is not guaranteed. This is primarily the reason why the *Locally Redundant Storage (LRS) option is recommended for data disks hosting SQL Server database files.* Another aspect to keep in mind is that LRS storage has twice the ingress/egress bandwidths of its peer categories like Geo-Redundant Storage/Zone Redundant Storage.

The first automation check is to use the virtual machine properties and compare the location of the compute and storage and ensure that it is co-located. The way to automate this is to retrieve the storage profile of the data disks attached to the virtual machine and determine if replication is enabled for them. The PowerShell script in Listing 7-2 assumes that the storage accounts in the resource group are associated with the SQL Server instance deployed in the same resource group. Its checks to see if storage replication is enabled and if storage and compute are co-located.

Listing 7-2. PowerShell Script for Storage Best Practices

```
$Accounts = @() #Empty list to store the account names

# Get the details about the virtual machine
$VM = Get-AzureRmVM -ResourceGroupName $RGName -Name $VMName

# Retrieve the URI from the virtual hard disks attached to the VM
$VHDs = $VM.StorageProfile.DataDisks.VirtualHardDisk.Uri
```

```
# Retrieve the storage account from each URI
foreach ($vhd in $VHDs)
{
    $Accounts = $Accounts + ((($vhd -split "//")[1]) -split ".blob")[0]
}
# Get the unique storage accounts
$Accounts = $Accounts | select -Unique

# Get the best practices for the account
foreach ($Account in $Accounts)
{
    $StorageAccount = Get-AzureRmStorageAccount -ResourceGroupName $RGName
    -Name $Account
    Write-Host "***** Storage account check for " $StorageAccount.
    StorageAccountName
    if ($StorageAccount.AccountType.ToString().Contains("LRS"))
    {
        Write-Host "[INFO] Replication is not enabled for the storage
        account" -ForegroundColor Green
    }
    else
    {
        Write-Host "[ERR] Account Type: " $StorageAccount.AccountType
        -ForegroundColor Red
        Write-Host "[ERR] It is recommended to disable any form of
        replication for your storage account" -ForegroundColor Red
    }

    if ($VM.Location -eq $StorageAccount.Location.Replace(" ",""))
    {
        Write-Host "[INFO] Storage and Compute are co-located"
        -ForegroundColor Green
    }
    else
    {
        Write-Host "[ERR] Storage and Compute are co-located" -ForegroundColor Red
    }
}
```

Data Disks

When you think about SQL Server database files and operating system disks, a few best practices do jump out irrespective of the platform and environment. *It is never a good idea to mix data and log files in the same volume and, in the case of Azure VMs, on the same data disks.* SQL Server data files thrive on random IO whereas transaction logs perform sequential IO. Due to the different IO profiles, the storage medium cannot perform optimally when both data and logs are performing large amounts of operations in short periods.

With Azure disks, there is a warm-up effect that can result in a reduced rate of throughput and bandwidth for a short period of time. In situations where a data disk is not accessed for a period of time (approximately 20 minutes), adaptive partitioning and load balancing mechanisms kick in. If the disk is accessed while these algorithms are active, you may notice some degradation in throughput and bandwidth for a short period of time (approximately 10 minutes), after which they return to their normal levels. This warm-up effect happens because of the adaptive partitioning and load balancing mechanism of Azure, which dynamically adjusts to workload changes in a multi-tenant storage environment. When deciding on the placement of your files on data disks, it is important to keep this information in mind.

The operating system disk is locally attached disk and not in the same performance class as required for hosting high performance, low latency database files. *It is advisable not to store anything on the operating system files other than, as the name suggests, operating system files.* All Azure Virtual Machines deployed from the gallery have C: as the operating system drive. Listing 7-3 shows a code sample used to check if database files are hosted on the operating System drive.

Listing 7-3. PowerShell Script To Test If Any Database Files Are Hosted on the Operating System [C:] Drive

```
$RulePass = 1
$sqlquery = "select distinct substring(physical_name,1,2) as drive from sys.
master_files where substring(physical_name,2,1) = ':'"
$sqlDrives = Invoke-Sqlcmd -ServerInstance $sqlserver -Query $sqlquery

# Find out the OS Drive
$Name = Get-WmiObject -Class Win32_DiskDrive -Filter "InterfaceType =
`"IDE`" " and SCSITargetId = 0" | Select-Object PAth
$Dependent = Get-WmiObject -Class Win32_DiskDriveToDiskPartition | Where-
Object {$_.Antecedent -contains $Name.Path} | Select-Object Dependent
$OSDrive = (Get-WmiObject -Class Win32_LogicalDiskToPartition | Where-
Object {$_.Antecedent -eq $Dependent.Dependent} | Select-Object Dependent).
Dependent.Split("`"")[1]

foreach ($drive in $sqlDrives)
{
    if ($drive.drive -eq $OSDrive)
    {
        Write-Host "[ERR] Database files found on OS drive" -ForegroundColor Red
        $RulePass = 0
    }
}

if ($RulePass -eq 1)
{
    Write-Host "[INFO] No database files found on OS drive" -ForegroundColor Green
}
```

The teams at Microsoft have tested various workloads on SQL Server running on Azure Virtual Machines and the verdict on the disk configuration is as follows (assuming that you are using Premium IO):

- *Enable read caching on the data disks that host data files and tempdb.* This allows reads and writes to be cached for future reads. The writes are persisted directly to Azure Storage to prevent data loss or data corruption while still enabling read cache. For transactional workloads, this is very beneficial.

- *Disable read caching for data disks that will host transaction log files.* This would bypass the cache completely. All disk transfers are completed against Azure Storage. This cache setting prevents the physical host local disks from becoming a bottleneck. This is a common problem with local disks, which manifests itself as `WRITELOG` or other IO-related waits when transaction log flushes are high. This configuration setting is very performant in scenarios where the rates of log flushes due to transaction commits are very high.

- *Temporary disk (typically D: drive) for certain tiers have locally attached SSDs.* Such disks can be used to host the tempdb or buffer pool extensions. Buffer pool extension was a feature added in SQL Server 2014, which targets non-volatile storage as an extension of the SQL Server buffer pool. See Listing 7-5 for a code sample that checks if the temporary drive is hosting database files other than tempdb.

- *Formatting the data disks with recommended allocation sizes (64KB).* This is especially beneficial for OLTP workload performance. (See Listing 7-4.)

A number of deployments have raised support incidents with Microsoft due to performance issues that have been attributed to these best practices not being followed.

Listing 7-4. PowerShell Code for Checking if the Allocation Unit Size Is Set to 64KB

```
function global:Split-Result()
{
param
(
[parameter(ValueFromPipeline=$true,
Mandatory=$true)]
[Array]$MATCHRESULT
)
```

```
process
{
$ReturnData=NEW-OBJECT PSOBJECT -property @{Title=";Value="}
$DATA=$Matchresult[0].tostring().split(":")
$ReturnData.Title=$Data[0].trim()
$ReturnData.Value=$Data[1].trim()
Return $ReturnData
}
}

$LogicalDisks = Get-WmiObject -Query "select * from Win32_LogicalDisk Where
MediaType = 12" | Select Name, MediaType, FileSystem, Size

foreach ($disk in $LogicalDisks)
{
    $Drive = $disk.Name + "\"
    $RESULTS=(fsutil fsinfo ntfsinfo $Drive)
    $AllocSize = $Results | Split-Result | Select-Object Title,Value |
    Where-Object {$_.Title -eq "Bytes Per Cluster"}
    if ($AllocSize.Value -eq 65536)
    {
        Write-Host "Allocation size for " $Drive " = " $AllocSize.Value " bytes"
        -ForegroundColor Green
    }
    else
    {
        Write-Host "Allocation size for " $Drive " = " $AllocSize.Value "
        bytes (Recommendation is 64K)" -ForegroundColor Red
    }
}
```

If you are not using Premium IO (Standard IO), caching should be disabled on all data disks. For production scenarios, it is recommended that you use Premium IO, as it is built for handling parallel, high queue depth IO workloads. Applications with highly concurrent and IO intensive workloads will see consistently high performance throughput.

Remember that testing is only as good as the environment. Benchmarking on low capability hardware gives low benchmarks and similarly benchmarking on low tier Azure VMs will provide inaccurate bottlenecks and benchmark numbers. The beauty of Azure is that you can turn off your test environment as soon as the test is completed and this lets you keep an eye out on the monthly bill without optimizing test quality. At the same time, you can maintain copies of the production environment at a fraction of the cost of what it would have been on-premises.

■ **Caution**   Hosting any other database files on the temporary drive will result in the database files being wiped to oblivion after the machine is shut down. Hosting database files other than tempdb on the temporary drive is a very quick and proven way to get a DBA's resume updated!

Listing 7-5. PowerShell Code to Check if Files Are Hosted on the Temporary Drive

```
$RulePass = 1
$sqlquery = "select distinct substring(physical_name,1,2) as drive,db_
name(database_id) as dbname, name, physical_name from sys.master_files where
substring(physical_name,2,1) = ':'"
$sqlDrives = Invoke-Sqlcmd -ServerInstance $sqlserver -Query $sqlquery
$Files = $sqlDrives | Where-Object {$_.drive -eq $TempDrive -and $_.dbname -ne
"tempdb"}

foreach ($file in $Files)
{
    Write-Host "[ERR] Database file" $file.name "(physical file:" $file.
    physical_name ") for database" $file.dbname "is hosted on the temporary
    drive" -ForegroundColor Red
    $RulePass = 0
}

if ($RulePass -eq 1)
{
    Write-Host "[INFO] No files found on the temporary drive" $TempDrive
    -ForegroundColor Green
}
else
{
    Write-Host "[ERR] Any data stored on" $TempDrive "drive is SUBJECT TO
    LOSS and THERE IS NO WAY TO RECOVER IT." -ForegroundColor Red
    Write-Host "[ERR] Please do not use this disk for storing any personal
    or application data." -ForegroundColor Red
}
```

Storage Spaces

Storage spaces are common configuration patterns used during the VM provisioning. If more than one disk is required for your specified settings, the latest gallery image templates create one Windows storage space (virtual drive) across all disks. A thought might have crossed your mind about the necessity to complicate the configuration. A number of databases hosted on-premises have a single database file that cannot be split evenly into multiple files at the drop of a hat. This might be due to the lack of partitioned data, which would could possibly make a single file the hotspot.

111

If you are using Windows Server 2012 or above, you can use storage spaces to group two or more drives together in a storage pool and then use capacity from that pool to create virtual drives called storage spaces. This feature of Windows allows you to absolve yourself from the need to split your database into multiple files. However, there are a few quirks that you need to be aware of.

The first quirk to remember is to configuring the number of columns correctly for the storage pool. Increasing the number of columns can significantly improve performance for sequential workloads. Random workloads do not experience as significant a performance increase, exhibiting more uniform performance across different column counts. Another factor that ties in directly with the column count of the space is the amount of outstanding IOs or data that is to be read from or written to the storage space. A large number of columns benefits applications that generate enough load to saturated multiple disks, but introduce unnecessary limitations on capacity expansion for less demanding applications. If there are more than eight data disks, you need to use PowerShell scripts to adjust the number of columns appropriately, as shown in Listing 7-6.

The second quirk to remember is the Resiliency setting. Storage spaces offer three resiliency settings: simple, parity, and mirror. If you select mirror, your data disk will end up performing two IO operations for a single IO generated by the SQL Server instance. Mirroring is recommended for resiliency, which can eat up your IO bandwidth on Azure. If you are only concerned about protecting the virtual machine from disk failures, this is already done under the hood by Azure Storage (details in Chapter 3), where redundant copies of the blobs hosting the data files are created by default.

Listing 7-6. PowerShell Script Example to Create a Virtual Disk Storage Pool with a Column Count of 2 and Simple Resiliency Setting

```
New-VirtualDisk -StoragePoolFriendlyName CompanyData -FriendlyName
BusinessCritical -ResiliencySettingName simple -Size 1TB -ProvisioningType
Thin -NumberOfColumns 2 -Interleave 65536
```

Tempdb

SQL Server's temporary database has been the victim of poorly optimized queries that spill over operations to the tempdb. The performance problems that plague tempdb are not a unique issue isolated to Azure VM. Tempdb performance is a source of constant headache if configured incorrectly. To ensure that your tempdb stays happy, enable trace flag 1118 (-T1118) to prevent resource allocation contention during the creation of temp objects by concurrent threads.

It is a good idea to increase the number of data files in tempdb to maximize disk bandwidth and to reduce contention in allocation structures. *As a general rule, if the number of logical processors is less than or equal to eight, use the same number of data files as logical processors.* If the number of logical processors is greater than eight, use eight data files. If contention continues, increase the number of data files by multiples of four (up to the number of logical processors) until the contention is reduced to acceptable levels or make changes to the workload/code. If your virtual machine's temporary drive is a SSD, hosting the tempdb on the temporary disk is recommend to increase performance throughput.

Figure 7-1 shows clearly that when the tempdb is hosted on standard disks, the performance is not consistent and the latency for certain IOs could be very high. This would lead to erratic performance, which would be unpalatable for mission- or business-critical workloads. When hosting the tempdb on SSD or Premium IO disks, the performance is consistent and the deviations are negligible.

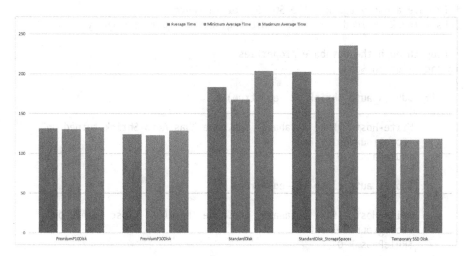

Figure 7-1. Tempdb performance comparison of SSD, Premium IO, and standard disks

In summary, if your application likes consistent tempdb performance, picking the SSD or Premium IO is the best bet.

Database Settings

The earlier sections talked in detail about how knowing your IO patterns and the IO bandwidth required helps you deploy the Azure VM with the correct configuration. This in turn allows you to get the best bang for your buck! There are also a few database level settings that help optimize for good performance throughput.

Database page compression helps reduce the IO, which is true for all environments but in Azure it definitely helps boost the performance for chatty systems.

If you are an avid reader of blogs, you would have seen multiple SQL Server professionals discouraging the use of Auto Shrink and Auto Close for a database; this is also true for databases hosted on SQL Server instances running on Azure VMs. Listing 7-7 shows how to determine if AUTO CLOSE and AUTO SHRINK are enabled for any database hosted on a SQL Server instance.

Listing 7-7. PowerShell Code to Determine if AUTO CLOSE and AUTO SHRINK Are Enabled on Any Database

```
$RulePass = 1
$sqlquery = "select name, is_auto_shrink_on, is_auto_close_on from sys.databases"

# Execute a query against the SQL Server instance
$dbs = Invoke-Sqlcmd -ServerInstance $sqlserver -Query $sqlquery

# Loop through the database properties
foreach ($db in $dbs)
{
    if ($db.is_auto_shrink_on -eq $true)
    {
        Write-Host "[ERR] Database" $db.name "has Auto Shrink turned on"
        -ForegroundColor Red
        $RulePass = 0
    }
    if ($db.is_auto_close_on -eq $true)
    {
        Write-Host "[ERR] Database" $db.name "has Auto Close turned on"
        -ForegroundColor Red
        $RulePass = 0
    }
}

if ($RulePass -eq 1)
{
    Write-Host "[INFO] No databases found with Auto Close and Auto Shrink
    turned on" -ForegroundColor Green
}
```

A few housekeeping tasks that you may need to perform after SQL Server is installed on your virtual machine are:

1. Change the default location of the database data and log files to ensure that new database files are hosted on the data disks attached to the virtual machine that were configured for hosting SQL Server database files.

2. Move the system database files to the data disks.

3. Move your error log, trace file locations, and extended events file targets to the data disks.

Service Account Privileges

There has been an eternal debate on the web about enabling the "lock pages in memory" privilege for the SQL Server service account. Lock pages in memory is a Windows policy that determines which account can use a process to keep memory allocations pinned in physical memory. It prevents the system from paging the data to virtual memory on disk. When the SQL Server service account is granted this user right, buffer pool memory cannot be paged out by Windows. For SQL Server instances running on Azure VMs, it is recommended that you provide the lock pages in memory security privilege to the SQL Server service account. This prevents the working set of the SQL Server process to get paged to disk. The biggest downside to the obvious performance hit of getting paged is that the page file of the virtual machine by default resides on the locally attached disks. Listing 7-8 shows how to determine if the lock pages in memory security privilege is granted to the SQL Server service account.

■ **Note**   Always remember to cap MAX SERVER MEMORY for the SQL Server instance, especially when enabling the lock pages in memory security privilege for the SQL Server service account.

Listing 7-8. PowerShell Script to Determine if Lock Pages in Memory Privilege Is Granted to the SQL Server Service Account

```
$RulePass = 1
$sqlquery = "SELECT locked_page_allocations_kb FROM sys.dm_os_process_memory"

# Execute a query against the SQL Server instance
$lpim = Invoke-Sqlcmd -ServerInstance $sqlserver -Query $sqlquery

if ($lpim.locked_page_allocations_kb -eq "0")
{
        Write-Host "[WARN] Lock Pages in Memory security privilege is not
        granted to the SQL Server service account" -ForegroundColor Red
        $RulePass = 0
}
if ($RulePass -eq 1)
{
    Write-Host "[INFO] Lock Pages in Memory Security Privilege is granted to
    the SQL Server service account" -ForegroundColor Green
}
```

Another easy performance win is to grant the SQL Server service account the "Performance Volume Maintenance Tasks" security privilege. When the SQL Server service account has this privilege, it allows the SQL Server to perform *instant file initialization*. This allows SQL Server to create data files without having to zero out the pages. If you do not have any security compliance requirement that prevents you from doing this, you should look at providing this security privilege to the SQL Server service account. Without this privilege, it can take as long as 10 times longer to create a database file! Figure 7-2 illustrates the difference between having and not having the privilege. Such an illustration is best left to this book and should not be determined in production environments. Listing 7-9 shows how to determine if the SQL Server service account has the privilege to perform instant file initialization for data files. It works for any instance of SQL Server.

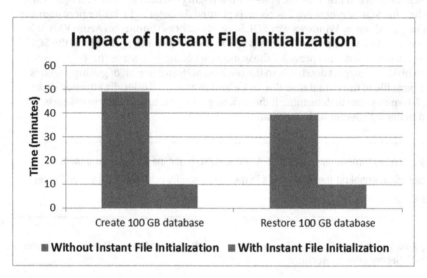

Figure 7-2. *Performance impact of instant file initialization*

Listing 7-9. PowerShell Script to Determine if the SQL Service Account Has the Ability to Perform Instant File Initialization

```
# Find out the SQL Server services installed on the machine
$SqlService = Get-WmiObject -Query "SELECT * FROM Win32_Service WHERE
PathName LIKE '%sqlservr%'"

# Export the secpol privileges on the machine to a file
$filename  = "secpol.inf"
$secpol = secedit /export /cfg $filename | Out-Null
$secpol = Get-Content $filename
# Search for the volumne maintenance task privilege in the output
$IFI = Select-String -Path $filename -Pattern "SeManageVolumePrivilege"
# Remove the file
#Remove-Item $filename

# Loop through each SQL Server service found on the machine
foreach ($servcice in $SqlService)
{
    # Find out the SID value of the service account
    $objUser = New-Object System.Security.Principal.NTAccount($servcice.StartName)
    $strSID = $objUser.Translate([System.Security.Principal.SecurityIdentifier])
```

```
# Find out if the SQL Service account SID exists in the output
if ($IFI.ToString().Contains($strSID.Value))
{
    Write-Host "[INFO] SQL Server service account ["$servcice.
    StartName"] has 'Perform Volume Maintenance Task' security
    privilege" -ForegroundColor Green
}
else
{
    Write-Host "[ERR] SQL Server service account ["$servcice.StartName"]
    has 'Perform Volume Maintenance Task' security privilege"
    -ForegroundColor Red
}
}
```

To take advantage of instant file initialization, you grant the SQL Server service account SE_MANAGE_VOLUME_NAME and add it to the Perform Volume Maintenance Tasks security policy. After adding the SQL Server service account to the Perform Volume Maintenance Tasks security policy, restart the SQL Server service.

Backups

One of the most common DBA tasks is to ensure that the data is backed up and protected from any sort of disaster. Protecting the data is a sacrosanct job that no DBA can refute. However, the art of backing up databases on an Azure VM is slightly different.

When you do configure the database backups, it is best to use SQL Server's Backup to Url feature (available in SQL Server 2012 Service Pack 1 Cumulative Update 2 or higher or SQL Server 2014 or SQL Server 2016), as it directly backs up to Azure blog storage. This is not something that you would have normally configured in data centers hosted on-premises, but is a no-brainer for your Azure VM. Another tip to keep in mind is to use the backup compression feature available in SQL Server. This leads to fewer numbers of network bytes transferred between your virtual machine and the blog store.

Figure 7-3 shows that there is a significant throughput and time difference between compressed backups to blob storage (denoted as the cloud) as opposed to uncompressed backups on the disk.

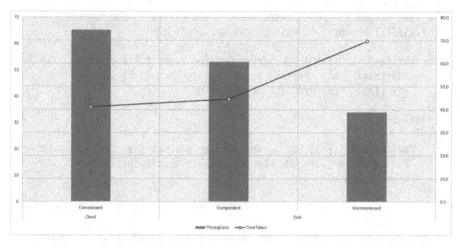

Figure 7-3. *Performance comparison of backing up to disk and to blob storage*

A glance at Figure 7-3 might make you wonder why there is a need to break the habit of backing up to a backup data disk if one is created for this purpose. On an Azure VM, the primary reason is that backing up to the disk consumes IOPs for your data disk and storage accounts, which have thresholds. You do not want to spend this commodity if it can be avoided, especially for high performance environments. If you concurrently back up multiple databases to a data disk, you could very quickly hit your disk throughput thresholds. And if you are using Premium IO disk for backups, this wouldn't be the best use of your resources and is counter-intuitive from a cost-benefit analysis! Listing 7-10 shows how to determine if backups of the databases are being stored on an Azure disk.

Listing 7-10. PowerShell Script to Check if Compressed Backups to Azure Blobs Are Being Performed on the SQL Server Instance

```
$sqlquery = "if exists (select TOP 1 physical_device_name from msdb.dbo.
backupmediafamily where physical_device_name not like 'http%')
        select 'Disk' as Result
else
        select 'Blob' as Result"

# Execute a query against the SQL Server instance
$backups = Invoke-Sqlcmd -ServerInstance $sqlserver -Query $sqlquery
# Check if backups are being done to BLOBs directly
if ($backups.Result -eq "Disk")
{
        Write-Host "[WARN] Database backups found on local disks"
        -ForegroundColor Red
        $RulePass = 0
}
```

```
if ($RulePass -eq 1)
{
    Write-Host "[INFO] All database backups are being backed up to Azure Blobs"
    -ForegroundColor Green
}

$sqlquery = "if exists (select top 1 backup_size from msdb.dbo.backupset
where compressed_backup_size = backup_size)
        select 'Uncompressed' as Result
else
        select 'Compressed' as Result"

# Execute a query against the SQL Server instance
$backups = Invoke-Sqlcmd -ServerInstance $sqlserver -Query $sqlquery
# Check if backups are being compressed or not
if ($backups.Result -eq "Uncompressed")
{
        Write-Host "[WARN] Uncompressed backups are being performed on this
        instance" -ForegroundColor Red
        $RulePass = 0
}
if ($RulePass -eq 1)
{
    Write-Host "[INFO] All database backups are using backup compression"
    -ForegroundColor Green
}
```

Data Files on Azure Blobs

SQL Server 2014 and above support an option to store your database files directly on Azure blobs. Since we already talked about breaking the habit in the earlier section, it might be worthwhile spending a few moments on this feature. This feature not only allows you to rid yourself of the need to attach additional data disks, but also allows you to leverage the limitless storage capacity of Azure blobs. This feature is available to a SQL Server instances running on an on-premises environment or an Azure VM. Using data files on Azure blobs frees you from the IOPs limits on data disks or a group of data disks. Especially on non-production environments, this is a great way to reduce the cost without affecting performance or compromising on IO performance consistency. This prevents the need of using Premium IO disks for your test environments.

Figure 7-4 illustrates the concept of hosting database files on Azure blobs.

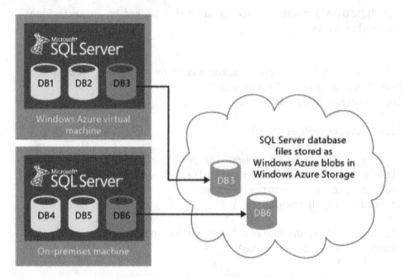

Figure 7-4. *SQL Server database files on Azure blobs*

The discussion of how SQL Server stores these files on Azure blobs is out-of-scope, but it's important to understand an added benefit of this feature. When you have data files hosted on Azure blob with SQL Server 2016, you have the option of leveraging SQL Server file-snapshot backup. This uses Azure snapshots to provide nearly instantaneous backups and quicker restores for database files stored using the Azure blob storage service. A file-snapshot backup (see Figure 7-5) consists of a set of Azure snapshots of the blobs containing the database files, plus a backup file containing pointers to these file-snapshots. Think SAN snapshots! Each file-snapshot is stored in the container with the base blob. You can specify that the backup file itself be written to URL, disk, or tape. However, backing up to URL is recommended. See Listing 7-11 for an example.

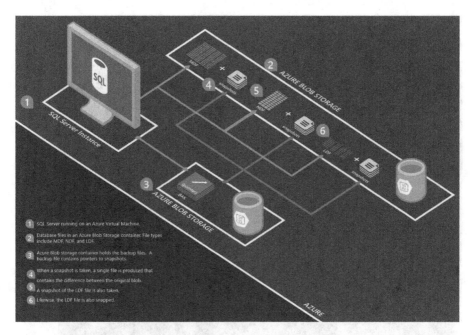

Figure 7-5. *File-snapshot backup of SQL Server databases using Azure blobs for data files*

Listing 7-11. Transact-SQL Example of File-Snapshot Backup

```
BACKUP DATABASE AdventureWorks2016
TO URL = 'https://<mystorageaccountname>.blob.core.windows.net/
<mycontainername>/AdventureWorks2016.bak'
WITH FILE_SNAPSHOT;
```

As you can see, storing the data files on Azure blobs and using file-snapshot backups greatly simplify your storage, backup, and restore story!

Monitoring

While we are on the topic of breaking the habit, it is important to note that almost all the data-gathering and analysis tools that you are used for on-premises or virtualized SQL Server instances work in pretty much similar fashion for SQL Server instances hosted on Azure VM. In the next few pages, you'll get acquainted with the new monitoring capabilities that Azure provides for SQL Servers running on Azure VMs.

One of the most common questions that you might face as a DBA is how to monitor performance of a SQL Server instance running on an Azure VM. One of the easiest answers is using the Azure portal. Figure 7-6 shows a customized set of tiles available on the virtual machine's landing page. You can add the groups and tiles to the view that you see in Figure 7-6.

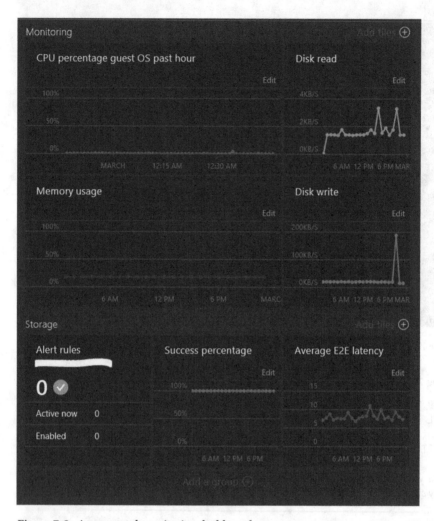

Figure 7-6. Azure portal monitoring dashboard

The portal lets you configure alerts on various perfmon counters that are available to be captured. Figure 7-7 shows the alert rules that are configured for a particular machine and also the actions that are available when the alert condition is met. A large number of the common alerts—such as disk, CPU, memory, network, and SQL performance counter-related thresholds—can be configured for a virtual machine. For the SQL performance metrics to be available, you have to enable SQL metrics to be collected under the Diagnostics tab (see Figure 7-7). This can be done during provisioning as well, which is explained in Chapter 5.

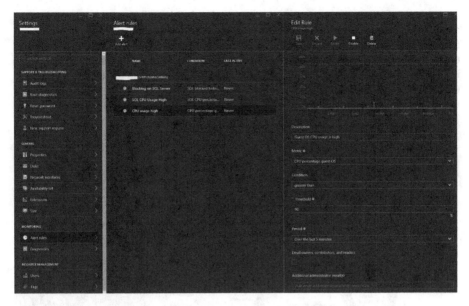

Figure 7-7. *Configuring performance-based alerts for a virtual machine*

If you want to get down to the factory approach of setting up the alerts for a large number of virtual machines, this is possible using canned scripts using the **Add-AlertRule** cmdlet. The response to the alert can be an e-mail and/or you can post the alert to a web hook, which can further process the alert.

Operational Insights

Some of the best practices checks are common to any SQL Server instance irrespective of the location. Since we are talking about SQL Server instances hosted on Azure Virtual Machines, this might be a prudent opportunity to discuss *Operational Insights*, which work for on-premises and Azure Virtual Machines.

Operational Insights, part of Microsoft Operations Management Suite, is a software as a service (SaaS) solution tailored to IT operations teams. This service uses the power of Azure to collect, store, and analyze log data from virtually any Windows Server and Linux source, from any data center or cloud, and turn that data into real-time operational intelligence to help you make better-informed decisions.

Figure 7-8 shows the Azure Operational Insights dashboard. This service provides a high value for various other benefits like enabling change tracking, capacity planning, malware assessment, etc., which show up as solutions in the Solutions Gallery. Although touching upon all the available solutions in the gallery is out-of-scope for this chapter, it's worthwhile to explore the solutions available in the gallery, even for a SQL Server environment!

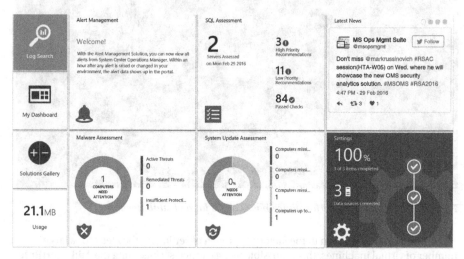

***Figure 7-8.** Azure Operational Insights home page showing enabled solutions*

To get started with Operational Insights, you need to download an agent that will have to be installed and configured with a workspace ID and a storage key, which will be used by the agent to upload the data to Azure. Once you have configured the agent, your first task is to enable the SQL Assessment solution. This provides a plethora of checks categorized under the following headings:

- Security and Compliance

- Availability and Business Continuity

- Performance and Scalability

- Upgrade, Migration, and Deployment

- Operations and Monitoring

- Change and Configuration Management

Depending on the data collected, your SQL Server instance might not report issues for certain categories and show up a bit red on certain others! Figure 7-9 shows the high and low priority recommendations for the different areas assessed.

Figure 7-9. SQL Assessment showing issues identfied in different areas

The tiles have additional drill-down capability that allows you to get additional information like the SQL Server instance that reported the issue, the affected object name, and additional reading material for the reported issue. You even get a recommended corrective action for the reported issue, as shown in Figure 7-10.

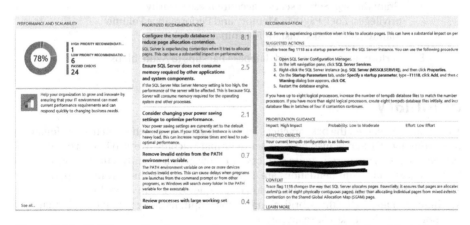

Figure 7-10. Drilldown of performance issues reported by Azure Operational Insights

The SQL Assessment checks a number of the post deployment performance considerations discussed earlier in this chapter, like tempdb configuration. This service has a free tier that has a retention period of seven days and a daily limit of 500MB per day. If you want to process more day with a higher retention period, especially with a large number of instances, you might need to leverage a paid tier for Operational Insights.

Cheat Sheet

If you felt this information was too much to digest in a short piece of time, here is a cheat sheet that you can use as a quick reference to set up your virtual machine hosting SQL Server.

1. Pick a minimum of DS3 for Enterprise Edition and DS2 for Standard Edition deployments. You might need to pick a higher virtual machine tier if you have high network bandwidth requirements.

2. Use Premium storage for high performance workloads and ensure that the compute and storage are co-located in the same region.

3. Disable geo-replication for the storage account.

4. Use separate P30 disks for hosting data, log, and tempdb files if required with an allocation unit size of 64K. Do not host data and log files on the same drive. Create a storage pool where necessary.

5. Enabled read caching for data and tempdb data disks and no caching for data disks hosting log files when using Premium storage. For Standard data disks, do not enable caching.

6. Disable AUTO CLOSE and AUTO SHRINK for the databases and prevent auto growth as much as possible.

7. Grant the SQL Server service account these security privileges: Lock Pages in Memory and Performance Volume Maintenance Tasks (Instant File Initialization).

8. Performance compressed database backups to Azure blobs.

Summary

This chapter explained the best practices and recommendations that you need to follow when running SQL Server instances on Azure Virtual Machine. We also looked options available in the Azure portal, Azure services, and PowerShell to verify if the performance best practices and recommendations are in place for the environment running SQL Server. Standard diagnostics data collection techniques work with Azure Virtual Machines, but leveraging the hybrid, cloud-enabled options along with the hooks that the new portal provides makes life a lot easier.

When you run the best practices check available in the GitHub repository (SqlOnAzureVM), you'll see the output in Figure 7-11.

```
 6   # Find out the temporary drive as it is needed for other checks
 7   $TempDrive = & '.\Temporary Drive.ps1'
 8   # Check if the correct VM size is being used
 9   Write-Host "***** Check for storage best practices"
10   &'.\Get-AllocationUnitCheck.ps1'
11   &'.\Get-StorageAccountBP.ps1' $VMName $RGName
12   &'.\Get-VMSize.ps1' $VMName $RGName
13   &'.\Get-IFI.ps1'
14   &'.\Get-LPIM.ps1' $sqlserver
15   Write-Host "***** Check for database properties"
16   &'.\Get-OSFilesDB.ps1' $sqlserver
17   &'.\Get-DBProperties.ps1' $sqlserver
18   &'.\Get-FilesOnTemp.ps1' $sqlserver $TempDrive
```

```
[INFO] Temporary drive on the machine is: D:
***** Check for storage best practices
Allocation size for  C:\  =  4096  bytes (Recommendation is 64K)
Allocation size for  D:\  =  4096  bytes (Recommendation is 64K)
Allocation size for  E:\  =  65536  bytes
Allocation size for  F:\  =  65536  bytes
Allocation size for  G:\  =  65536  bytes
Allocation size for  H:\  =  65536  bytes
Allocation size for  I:\  =  65536  bytes
***** Storage account check for  bigtigerdojo
[INFO] Replication is not enabled for the storage account
[INFO] Storage and Compute are co-located
***** Storage account check for  tigerdojo
[INFO] Replication is not enabled for the storage account
[INFO] Storage and Compute are co-located
[INFO] Virtual machine size:  Standard_DS3
[INFO] SQL Server service account [ NT Service\MSSQLSERVER ] has 'Perform Volume Maintenance Task' security privilege
[WARN] Lock Pages in Memory security privilege is not granted to the SQL Server service account
***** Check for database properties
[INFO] No database files found on OS drive
[INFO] No databases found with Auto Close and Auto Shrink turned on
[INFO] No files found on the temporary drive D:
```

Figure 7-11. *Result of a best practices check executed on an Azure Virtual Machine hosting SQL Server*

127

CHAPTER 8

■ ■ ■

Azure SQL Database

Microsoft Azure SQL Database is a relational database service in Microsoft Azure based on the Microsoft SQL Server engine, with almost all the mission-critical capabilities of SQL Server. Windows Azure SQL Database is designed to deliver highly available and scalable database as a service with predictable performance, business continuity, and data protection capabilities. SQL Database is a platform as a server offering, and it requires very little administrative overhead and can significantly reduce the time-to-market for applications requiring database backend support. Since the service is based on the SQL Server engine, it works with most of the SQL Server tools and APIs available, making it easier to migrate existing applications to Azure.

In this chapter, we will learn about the internal architecture of Azure SQL Database and how the Windows Azure Fabric plays an important role in the management and functioning of the Azure SQL Database. We will learn about the various service tiers and performance levels available with the Azure SQL Database and the management features or options available to manage an Azure SQL database.

We will also learn about the different techniques that can be utilized to migrate an on-premises database to an Azure SQL database.

SQL Database Architecture

Azure SQL Database is built on top of the Windows Azure framework, which provides machine management and distributed application functionality. A SQL Azure cluster consists of a control ring and one or more tenant rings. In Windows Fabric terminology, each ring equates to a physical Windows Azure cluster that consists of a collection of nodes that run one or more applications. Each application within a ring contains one or more services.

The Tenant Ring

A tenant ring in the Windows Fabric is nothing but a physical Windows Azure cluster, where each node of the cluster is designed to run an application. In this case, the application being run is of type DBService, which is basically a SQL Server engine service or the Hekaton (in-memory OLTP) engine service. Each DBService application is bound to its own memory, CPU, and IO.

© Pranab Mazumdar, Sourabh Agarwal, Amit Banerjee 2016
P. Mazumdar et al., *Pro SQL Server on Microsoft Azure*, DOI 10.1007/978-1-4842-2083-2_8

When customers provision an Azure SQL Database, they create a logical server (if it doesn't already exist) and a database. They are actually creating a DBService (or DBSvc) in the backend. This DBService application runs on one of the nodes of the Windows Azure cluster. The DBService can use the local storage on the VM (or the host) and remote storage (see Figure 8-1) for storing the database.

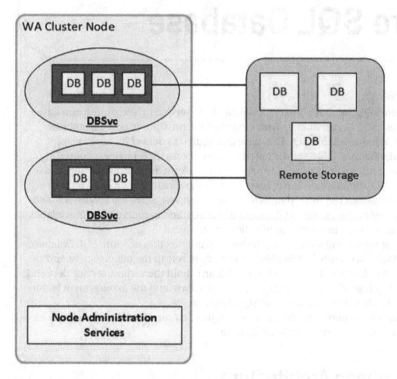

Figure 8-1. *DBService running on Windows Azure clusters*

The tenant ring architecture allows for the creation and functioning of multiple DBServices, belonging to one or more customers (tenants). Since each DBService runs in its own context and is independent of other DBService applications running on the same node in the tenant ring, this architecture allows the same node/VM to host multiple customer databases.

The following services form the core of the DBService application:

- SQL Server Executable

- Watchdog.exe

There might be additional services when Hekaton (in-memory OLTP) or full text is also required. Additionally, there might be other services that are needed when Azure SQL Database forms the backend to Azure SQL DW.

The Control Ring

The control ring functions to provide management, provisioning, and redirecting services (see Figure 8-2). It helps determine the location of the databases in the tenant rings and routing connections to the right tenant databases. Control ring provides the following major services: Control Management Nodes, Management Services Nodes, and Redirector Services Nodes.

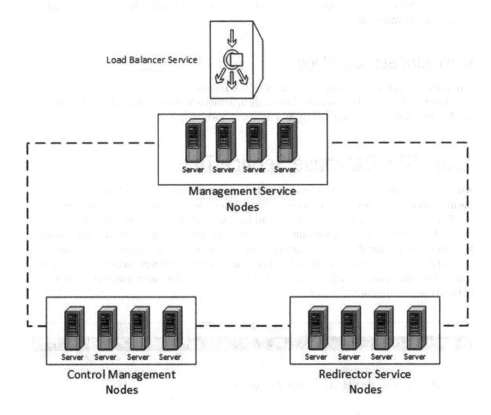

Figure 8-2. Control ring architecture

Control Management Node

The control management node provides internal cluster management services that provide capabilities like capacity management, tenant ring management, migration, and other such scenarios.

One of the key components of the control management node is the cluster metadata store, which is the single point of all metadata related to the Azure SQL clusters. It stores information such as the state of the cluster, the state of the resources running on the cluster, and other information that's ensures that the cluster is functioning optimally.

131

Management Service Node

The management services node hosts management components that provide REST APIs for management of the Azure SQL database by the end users. The management services run as stateless services on multiple active management nodes. If a node fails, the service can be restarted on a different management node and the operation can resume from the same point when the node hosting the service failed. The incoming end user requests host one of the various management endpoints and are then redirected to a management node by a software load balancer.

Redirector Services Node

This provides TDS redirection to the Azure SQL database.

The architecture also uses other services to achieve high availability (SQL Server availability groups), load balancing, and resource governance.

Azure SQL Database Service Tiers

Azure SQL Database is currently available in three service tiers with multiple performance levels, available under each service tier. For example, the standard tier has four performance levels—S0, S1, S2, and S3. Each performance level provides an increasing set of resources (compute power, memory, and storage) to provide increasing level throughput. The different service tiers and the various performance levels under each of the tiers are shown in Figure 8-3. Given that Azure is an ever-changing landscape, some of the information might change in the future. Up-to-date information can be found in the Azure document on MSDN.

	Basic	Standard				Premium				
Performance Level		S0	S1	S2	S3	P1	P2	P4	P3/P6	P11
DTU's	5	10	20	50	100	125	250	500	1000	1750

Figure 8-3. *Service tiers for Azure SQL Database*

The resources available under each performance level are expressed in terms of Database Throughput Units (or DTUs). In very simple terms, DTUs describes the relative amount of compute power, memory, and IO throughput required to complete a database transaction. For example, the standard S2 performance level provides 50 DTUs of computational power, which equates to ~50 database transactions per second. Similarly, the P11 service tier provides 1750 DTUs and can perform ~1750 transactions per second.

When migrating from on-premises environments to an Azure SQL Database, you can use a publicly available (non-Microsoft) DTU throughput calculator to estimate the number of DTUs and consequently determine the service tier that might be required for your workload. The DTU calculator can be downloaded from http://dtucalculator. azurewebsites.net/. See Figure 8-4.

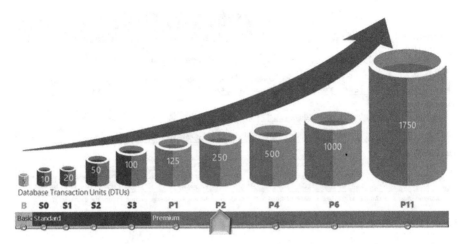

Figure 8-4. *Database Throughput Units (DTUs) across various service tiers and performance levels*

Elastic Database Pool

Azure SQL Database also allows for creation and management of multiple databases in an Elastic Database Pool. To understand Elastic Database Pool in more details, consider an example.

Let's say there is an ISV that provides SaaS (software as a service) services to multiple customers. For each of the customers, this ISV has to provision a database to be used as the backend of the software service. Each of these customers has varying peak usage times and requirements. Let's say for a customer A, the peak usage varies from 200 connections per second to 1000 connection per second. This variation in load might not be bound to specific times of the day. Under such circumstances it becomes difficult to provision a database, under a single service tier, which would allow optimal performance and be cost effective at the same time. Since the user load may not be time-dependent, the ISV will more likely have to provision a database with the highest service tier, which meets the peak load requirements. This obviously is not a cost-effective solution.

Elastic Database Pool provides a solution for such problems. In simple terms, Elastic Database Pool provides a set of shared DTUs (eDTUs to be more precise) associated with the pool, which can be utilized by the databases in the pool. For example, consider a standard S3 tier of elastic pool that has about 800 DTUs. A user can create a maximum of 400 databases in this pool, which would allow these databases to share and consume DTU resources without needing to assign a specific performance level to the databases in the pool. The arrangement allows multiple databases with varying workloads to optimally use the available DTUs in the pool. Figure 8-5 provides a listing of various limits for elastic pool in the different service tiers.

ELASTIC POOL LIMITS	Basic					Standard					Premium				
eDTUs per pool	100	200	400	800	1,200	100	200	400	800	1,200	125	250	500	1,000	1,500
Max. storage*	10 GB	20 GB	39 GB	78 GB	117 GB	100 GB	200 GB	400 GB	800 GB	1.2 TB	63 GB	125 GB	250 GB	500 GB	750 GB
Max. DBs	200		400			200		400					50		
Max. concurrent workers	200	400	800	1,600	2,400	200	750	1,300	1,850	2,400	200	750	1,300	1,850	2,400
Max. concurrent sessions	2,400	4,800	9,600	19,200	28,800	2,400	4,800	9,600	19,200	28,800	2,400	4,800	9,600	19,200	28,800

ELASTIC DB LIMITS	Basic	Standard	Premium
Max. storage*	2 GB	250 GB	500 GB
Min. eDTUs	0, 5	0, 10, 20, 50, 100	0, 125, 250, 500, 1000
Max. eDTUs	5	10, 20, 50, 100	125, 250, 500, 1000

BUSINESS CONTINUITY			
Point-in-time restore	Any point last 7 days	Any point last 14 days	Any point last 35 days
Disaster recovery	Geo-restore, restore to any Azure region	Standard geo-replication, offline secondary	Active geo-replication, up to four readable secondary backups

*Databases share pool storage, so database storage is limited to the smaller of remaining pool storage or max. storage per database.

Figure 8-5. *Elastic pool limits for various service tiers*

Service Tiers: Limits and Capabilities

Each of the services tiers available with the Azure SQL Database has specific limits, some of which are mentioned in Figure 8-6 and in the following list. Again, as mentioned earlier, updated information can be found in the Azure Documentation on MSDN.

	Basic	Standard				Premium				
		S0	S1	S2	S3	P1	P2	P4	P6/P3	P11
Maximum database size	2 GB	250 GB				500 GB				1 TB
DTUs	5	10	20	50	100	125	250	500	1,000	1,750
Point-in-time restore	Any point last 7 days	Any point last 14 days				Any point last 35 days				
Disaster recovery	Geo-Restore, restore to any Azure region	Standard Geo-Replication, offline secondary				Active Geo-Replication, up to 4 online (readable) secondary backups				
Max In-Memory OLTP storage	NA	NA	NA	NA	NA	1 GB	2 GB	3 GB*	8 GB	10 GB*
Max concurrent requests	30	60	90	120	200	200	400	800	1,600	2,400
Max concurrent logins	30	60	90	120	200	200	400	800	1,600	2,400
Max sessions	300	600	900	1,200	2,400	2,400	4,800	9,600	19,200	32,000

* In-Memory OLTP storage limits will soon adjust to 4 for P4 and 14 for P11.

Figure 8-6. *Service tiers capabilities and limits*

- *Maximum Database Size.* Specifies the max size limit on the database. As mentioned in the table, the maximum limit for a basic tier database is 2GB, while the max for a Premium P11 database is 1TB.

- *Automatic Backups and Point-In-Time Restore.* Azure SQL Database provides automatic full and log backup features. These backups can be restored to any point in time in the retention period as specified by the service tiers. For example, the standard tier DB backups are retained for 14 days by default and hence can be restored to any point in time in the last 14 days. We will be covering high availability, business continuity, and disaster recovery in full in the Chapter 9.

- *Max In-Memory OLTP Storage.* Specifies the maximum amount of storage allowed for storing in-memory OLTP objects. This is only applicable for premium tiers since the other tiers do not support in-memory OLTP optimizations.

- *Max Concurrent Requests.* The maximum number of concurrent user or application requests that can execute on the database. Readers familiar with Microsoft SQL Server might remember that SQL Server exposes a DMV `sys.dm_exec_requests`, which lists all the active requests running on the server. Similar DMVs can be used with WASD to get the total number of requests active on the database at any point in time.

- *Max Concurrent Logins.* This represents the limit of the number of users or applications allowed to log in to the database at the same time. This limit is not applicable to Elastic Database Pool.

Management Tools

Management (creation, updating, migration, etc.) of Azure SQL Database can be done with any of the following tools:

- Azure Portal
- SQL Server Management Studio
- SQL Server data tools
- Command-line utilities and REST APIs

These are discussed in the next sections.

Azure Portal

Azure Portal is a web based application that provides capabilities to create, delete, restore, and manage Azure SQL Database and the associated logical server. It also provides capabilities to monitor database performance, configure security and high availability, and the ability to change the service tier of the database.

Let's look at a couple of important tasks that can be done using Azure Portal: creating databases and managing database properties.

Create Database

When creating the database using Azure Portal (this example uses the New Azure Portal), we get the choice of choosing an existing server or creating a new logical server. If a new server is being created as part of the DB creation, users have the option to choose the data center in which the server and the database will reside. (See Figure 8-7, which indicates that the new database would be created on a logical server `tnkl47icl` in the Southeast Asia data center.)

135

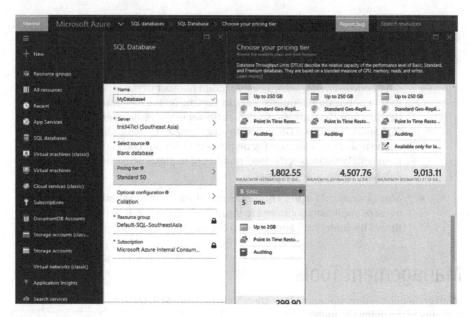

Figure 8-7. *Choosing the service tier and performance level while creating a new SQL database*

Users can also choose the service tier and the performance level of the database being created, as illustrated in Figure 8-7. The service tier and the performance level of a database can be changed using the Management portal, after creating the database.

Managing Database Properties

Azure Portal can be used to enable, disable, or change the properties of the database. As illustrated in Figure 8-8, the Azure Portal can also be used to restore, export, change the service tier, and enable or disable auditing and monitoring on the database.

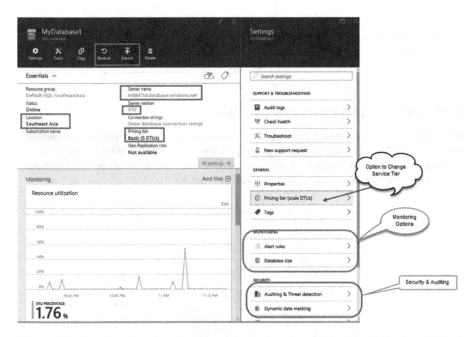

Figure 8-8. *Database details and management options available through the Azure Portal*

One of the most important uses of the Azure Portal is to configure firewall exceptions for connections from client IPs. Azure by default blocks all incoming traffic to the SQL database. An exception should be added before the database can be accessed by any of the client tools like SQL Server Management Studio (SSMS) or SQL Server Data Tools (SSDT).

This setting is performed at the server level, as illustrated in Figure 8-9.

Figure 8-9. *Configuring firewall options for an Azure SQL database server*

■ **Note**   Auditing, security, monitoring, high availability, and performance troubleshooting
are covered in the later chapters.

SQL Server Management Studio

SQL Server Management Studio, a very well-known management utility available with SQL
Server since 2005, can be utilized to manage and perform development of the Azure SQL
Database. As illustrated in Figure 8-10, SSMS can be used to connect to the Azure SQL Database
and perform management or other operations on the database.

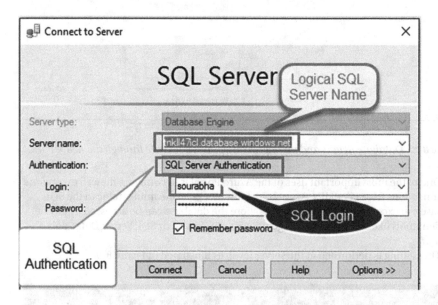

Figure 8-10.   Connecting to SQL Database using SQL Server Management Studio (SSMS)

Azure SQL databases support both SQL Authentication and Windows Authentication
(when using AD federation between on-premises AD and an Azure AD).

When connecting to Azure SQL Database, you need to specify the name of the logical
SQL Server created as part of the database creation. The name of the logical SQL Server
database is always in the format shown in Figure 8-10.

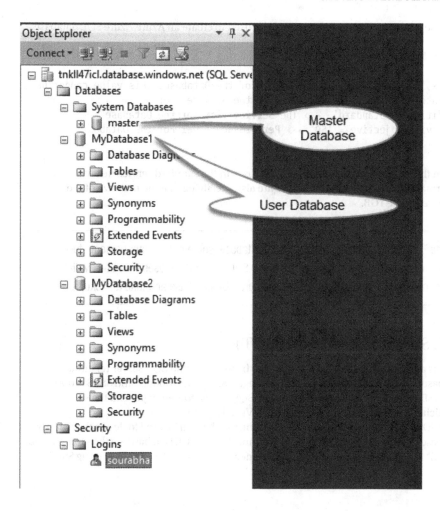

<LogicalServerName>.database.windows.net

Figure 8-11. *Exploring SQL Database using SQL Server Management Studio*

SSMS can be utilized to perform a lot of activities, such as:

- Monitoring and management using Extended Events
- Database creation, design, and development
- Managing security

The following T-SQL command can be used to create an Azure Azure SQL database:

```
CREATE DATABASE MyTestDatabase3
(
    MaxSize = 1 GB, ---> Maximum Size of the Database. This value cannot be
    grater than the size supported by the Service Tier
    Edition = 'Standard', --> The Service Tier for the Database
    Service_Objective = 'S0' --> Performance Level For the Database.
)
```

In this example, we are creating a database in the standard service tier, with a performance level of S0 (10 DTUs). We are also specifying that the max size of the database will be 1GB.

■ **Note**   When connecting to Azure SQL Database, some of the management studio features or capabilities available with regular SQL Server databases won't be available. For example, you cannot right-click on an Azure SQL database and take a backup of it.

SQL Server Data Tools (SSDT)

SSDT is a free downloadable utility that can be used to build SQL Server relational databases, Azure SQL databases, SSIS packages, SSAS data models, and SSRS reports. With SSDT, you can design and deploy any SQL Server content type with the same simplicity as you develop an application in Visual Studio.

SSDT is primarily a development environment that can be used to design the Azure SQL Database. The connection strings used to connect to the SQL Database are the same as used with SSMS. Figure 8-12 illustrates how to connect to an Azure SQL Database using SSDT.

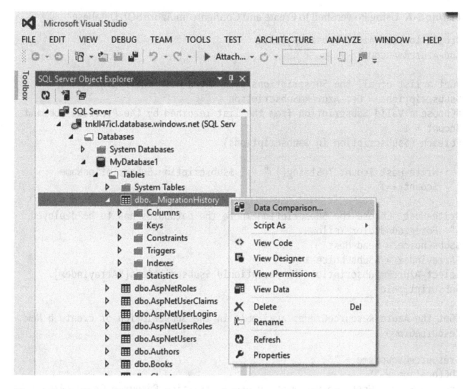

Figure 8-12. *Using SSDT to connect to and design an Azure SQL database*

Command-Line Utilities and REST APIs

Command-line utilities like PowerShell can be used to create and manage Azure SQL databases. Similarly, Azure exposes a set of REST APIs that can be utilized to work with Azure SQL databases.

PowerShell can be utilized to perform almost all operations related to an Azure SQL database. Listing 8-1 uses the Azure PowerShell cmdlets to perform the following tasks:

1. Log in to Azure.

2. Select a subscription to work with.

3. Select an existing ResourceGroup or create a new one. When you're creating a new ResourceGroup, the script allows users to select the data center.

4. Select an existing logical server or create a new one.

5. Configure the firewall rules to allow connections to the logical server from the client machine.

6. Configure the SQL Database. The script configures a database in the basic service tier.

Listing 8-1. Using PowerShell to Create and Configure an Azure SQL Database

```
#Login to your Azure Subscription.
Add-AzureRmAccount

#Get a list of all the Subscriptions associated with the login
$subscriptions = Get-AzureRmSubscription
#Choose a Valid Subscription from the list returned by the Previous Command
$count = 1
Foreach ($subscription in $subscriptions)
{
    Write-Host $count.ToString() " -:" $subscription.SubscriptionName
    $count +=1
}
Write-Host "Choose the Subscription where the databases has to be deployed
-" -ForegroundColor Yellow
$SubsChoice = Read-Host
$Arrayindex = $SubsChoice-1
Select-AzureRmSubscription -SubscriptionId $subscriptions[$Arrayindex].
SubscriptionId

#Get the Azure ResourceGroups available in the Subscription or create a New
ResourceGroup

$resourceGroupName = ""
$DCLocation = ""
$option = Read-Host "Do you want to use an existing Resource Group (y/n) :-"
if($option -eq "y")
{
    $ResGroups = Get-AzureRmResourceGroup | Where-Object{$_.
    ResourceGroupName -NotLike "Default*" }
    #Choose a Valid Subscription from the list
    $count = 1
    Foreach ($ResGroup in $ResGroups)
    {
        Write-Host $count.ToString() " -:" $ResGroup.ResourceGroupName
        $count +=1
    }
    Write-Host "Choose the ResourceGroup to which the databases has to be
    deployed -" -ForegroundColor Yellow
    $ResGrChoice = Read-Host
    $Arrayindex = $ResGrChoice-1
    $resourceGroupName = $ResGroups[$Arrayindex].ResourceGroupName
    $DCLocation = $ResGroups[$Arrayindex].Location
}
Else
{
```

```powershell
Write-Host "Enter the New ResourceGroup Name" -ForegroundColor Yellow
$resourceGroupName = Read-Host

$locations = Get-AzureLocation
$count=1
Foreach ($location in $locations)
{
    Write-Host $count.ToString() " -:" $location.Name
    $count +=1
}
Write-Host "Choose a Data Center Location " -ForegroundColor Yellow
$LocChoice = Read-Host
$Arrayindex = $LocChoice-1
$DCLocation = $locations[$Arrayindex].Name

try
{
    $resourceGroup = New-AzureRmResourceGroup -Name $resourceGroupName
    -Location $DCLocation
}
catch
{}
}

#Select either an existing logical server or create a new logical server for
the database.
$SQLDBServerName = ""
$option = Read-Host "Do you want to use an existing SQL Database Server
(y/n) :-"
if($option -eq "y")
{
    $logicalServers = Get-AzureRmSqlServer -ResourceGroupName
    $resourceGroupName
    #Choose a Valid SQLDatabase Server from the list
    $count = 1
    Foreach ($logicalServer in $logicalServers)
    {
        Write-Host $count.ToString() " -:" $logicalServer.ServerName
        $count +=1
    }
    Write-Host "Choose the Logical SQLDatabase Server where the databases
    has to be deployed -" -ForegroundColor Yellow
    $SrvChoice = Read-Host
    $Arrayindex = $SrvChoice-1
    $SQLDBServerName = $logicalServers[$Arrayindex].ServerName
}
```

```
Else
{
    Write-host "Enter the name for the SQL Server :-" -ForegroundColor Yellow
    $SQLDBServerName = Read-Host
    $SQLDBServerName = $SQLDBServerName.ToLower()
    $admin = Read-Host "Enter the Admin Account -:"
    $password =  Read-host "Enter the Admin Password -:" -assecurestring
    $Pscred = New-Object System.Management.Automation.PSCredential
    ($admin,$password)
    $DbServer = New-AzureRmSqlServer -ServerName $SQLDBServerName
-SqlAdministratorCredentials $Pscred -Location $DCLocation
-ResourceGroupName $resourceGroupName
}

#Add Firewall Rules to allow connections from the local machine
$FirewallRuleName = "Rule1"
$FirewallStartIP = "125.16.230.6"
$FirewallEndIp = "125.16.230.6"
$FirewallRule = New-AzureRmSqlServerFirewallRule -ResourceGroupName
$resourceGroupName -ServerName $SQLDBServerName -FirewallRuleName
$FirewallRuleName -StartIpAddress $FirewallStartIP -EndIpAddress
$FirewallEndIp

#Add the SQL Database
$DatabaseName = "MyDatabase2"
$DatabaseEdition = "Basic"
$DatabasePerfomanceLevel = "Basic"
$SqlDatabase = New-AzureRmSqlDatabase -ResourceGroupName $resourceGroupName
-ServerName $SQLDBServerName -DatabaseName $DatabaseName -Edition
$DatabaseEdition -RequestedServiceObjectiveName $DatabasePerfomanceLevel
```

Azure SQL Database versus SQL Server on Azure VM

One of the key decisions points for organization and Azure users is whether to deploy Azure SQL Database or SQL Server on Azure VMs for their relational database needs. Azure SQL Databases and SQL Server on Azure VM are optimized for different requirements.

Azure SQL Database is great in scenarios when there is a need to provision and manage many databases. Given that it's a PaaS offering, all the management and patching overhead is taken care of by the vendor, which helps organizations and users concentrate on just the design and usage of the database. Azure SQL databases are optimized for scenarios where there is a quick turnaround time (go-to market time) and lower cost requirements.

Azure SQL Databases do not provide all the peripheral features like replication, SQL Server Agent, etc., so for organizations that rely heavily on such features, Azure SQL Databases would not be a good option.

SQL Server on Azure VMs is optimized for scenarios where an organization is looking to extend its on-premises deployments to the cloud. Since the SQL Server engine running on an Azure VM is exactly the same as that running on your on-premises environments, it's easier for organizations to lift-and-shift their SQL workloads to Azure. With SQL Server running on Azure VMs, the organization's IT team has full administrative control over the VMs.

Table 8-1 summarizes the key differences between Azure SQL Database and SQL Server on Azure VMs.

Table 8-1. *Azure SQL Database vs. SQL Server on Azure VMs*

Feature	Azure SQL Databases	SQL Server on Azure VMs
Database size	Max 1TB available with P11 performance level.	Max database size constrained by the size of the VM. For example, on a D14 machine, you can have a maximum of 32 data disks, each of which is 1TB max. So theoretically, you can have a database that's 32TB.
Compute resources	No direct control over computing resources. Since the computing resources are represented as DTUs, the organization needs to performance benchmark their performance requirements.	Full control over the compute resources for the SQL Server deployments.
Cost of ownership	Completely eliminates the need for hardware or IT resources to manage the environment.	Eliminates the need for hardware requirements, but organizations still need to have an IT team to manage the VMs.
Business continuity	Provides the following by default: 1. Built-in fault tolerance and local (same data center) redundancy for high availability. 2. Automatic backups (retention period is dependent on the service tier). 3. Options such as geo-replication and point-in-time restore of the databases.	1. Azure infrastructure provides fault-tolerance and high availability for the VMs. 2. SQL level high-availability and disaster-recovery options need to be configured by the IT team. 3. Achieving high-availability often requires provisioning new VMs, which can increase the management and pathing overheads.

(continued)

Table 8-1. (*continued*)

Feature	Azure SQL Databases	SQL Server on Azure VMs
SQL engine features	Supports almost all the database level features available with traditional box SQL Server, but does not support peripheral features like SQL Server agent jobs, replication (only supported as a subscriber), log shipping, etc.	SQL Server on Azure VM is running the same SQL Server engine build as the traditional box product.
Usage scenarios	1. New cloud-designed applications that have time constraints in development and marketing. 2. Applications that need built-in high availability, disaster recovery, and upgrade mechanisms. 3. organizations or users who do not have the resources to manage the underlying operating system and configuration settings. 4. Building software as a service (SaaS) applications.	1. Organizations looking to migrate to the cloud with minimal changes to their existing applications. 2. Applications or workloads that require access to resources that are external to SQL Server. 3. Organizations that require full administrative rights on their SQL Server deployments. 4. As a DR deployment for on-premises SQL Server deployments.
Scalability	Easily scalable by changing the service tiers or the performance level of the database. This is an online operation, which means the database would be online and available while the change is being performed.	Can be scaled up by changing the base VM type. This is an offline operation and would enforce downtime for the SQL Servers.

Migrating to Azure SQL Database

Existing relational databases on either Microsoft SQL Server or on other RDBMS products like Oracle, DB2, etc. can be migrated to Azure SQL Database. When migrating from Microsoft SQL Server 2005 and above, you can use SQL Server Management Studio (SSMS) or SQL Server Data Tools (SSDT), whereas when migrating from non-Microsoft RDBMS products, you need to use the SQL Server Migration Assistant (SSMA) utility, which can be downloaded from Microsoft downloads.

For the remainder of this chapter, we talk about migrating an existing Microsoft SQL Server database to Azure SQL Database. Since Azure SQL Database does not support the full set of features available with SQL Server, it is very important to ensure that the existing database does not use features that are not supported on Azure SQL Database. You can check for this using either SQLPackage.exe or SSMS.

SQLPackage.exe

SQLPackage is a command-line utility available as part of the SQL Server or Visual Studio installation. The executable can be located in the following folders:

```
SQL Installations- C:\Program Files (x86)\Microsoft SQL Server\120\ DAC\bin
Visual Studio - C:\Program Files (x86)\Microsoft Visual Studio 12.0\Common7\
IDE\Extensions\Microsoft\SQLDB\DAC\120
```

The folders might vary depending on the version of SQL Server or Visual Studio installed on your server.

SQLPackage.exe supports the following actions (the complete documentation can be found at https://msdn.microsoft.com/library/hh550080.aspx):keez

1. *Extract.* Creates a database snapshot (*.dacpac) of a SQL Server or Azure SQL Database.

2. *Export.* Exports a database to a *.bacpac file.

3. *Import.* Imports a *.bacpac file to a database.

4. *Publish.* Publishes the contents of a .dacpac file to the target database.

5. *DeployReport.* Creates an XML report of the changes that would be made by a publish action.

6. *DriftReport.* Creates an XML report of the changes that have been made to a registered database since it was last registered.

7. *Script.* Creates a script of all the changes to be updated on the target database.

To get the list of potential issues that might block your efforts of migrating a database to Azure SQL Database, use the following command:

```
sqlpackage.exe /Action:Export /ssn:"SQLServerName" /sdn:"DatabaseName"
/tf:"Target Bacpac File" > "OutputFile" 2>&1
```

Where the parameter 2>&1 indicates that we want to log the errors and output in the same file.

Listing 8-2 shows sample output from the execution.

Listing 8-2. Output of SQLPackage.exe

```
Connecting to database 'SQLNexus' on server 'SQLServerName'.
Extracting schema
Extracting schema from database
Resolving references in schema model
Validating schema model
Validating schema model for data package
Validating schema
```

```
Exporting data from database
Exporting data
Processing Export.
Processing Table '[dbo].[tbl_PERF_STATS_SCRIPT_RUNTIMES]'.
Processing Table '[dbo].[tblNexusInfo]'.
Processing Table '[dbo].[tbl_BLOCKING_CHAINS]'.
Processing Table '[dbo].[tblDiagScan]'.
..........

Processing Table '[dbo].[tblDiagScanLookup]'.
Processing Table '[dbo].[CounterDetails]'.
Processing Table '[dbo].[tbl_RUNTIMES]'.
Processing Table '[dbo].[tbl_SYSINFO]'.
Processing Table '[dbo].[tbl_Reports]'.
Successfully exported database and saved it to file 'C: \Target.bacpac'.
```

In this case, there were no issues detected with the database.

SQL Server Management Studio

Using SQL Server Management Studio, users can create a bacpac file export of their database, as illustrated in Figures 8-13 through 8-15. The Export Data Tier Application option from SSMS can be utilized for creating a bacpac file for the existing on-premises database, which then can be imported as an Azure SQL Database. A bacpac file encapsulates both the data and schema of the database.

SSMS Export Data Tier Application allows users to choose which objects (tables, procedures, triggers, etc.) to include in the bacpac file.

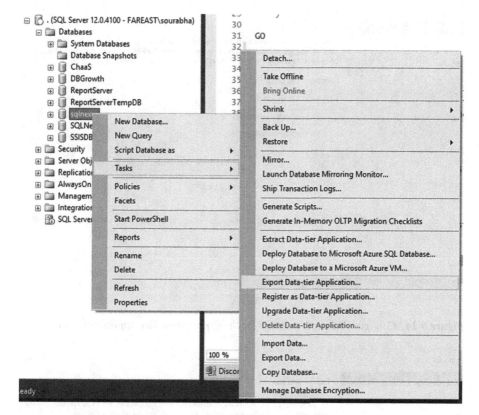

Figure 8-13. *Launching the Export Data Tier Application wizard in SSMS*

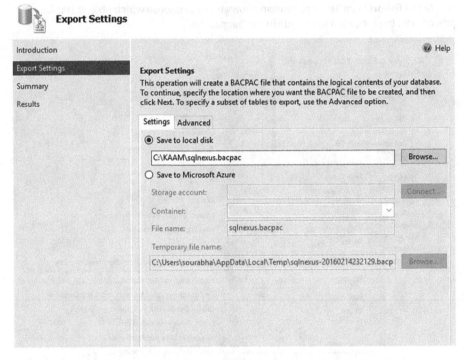

Figure 8-14. *Configure the export settings for the Export Data Tier Application wizard*

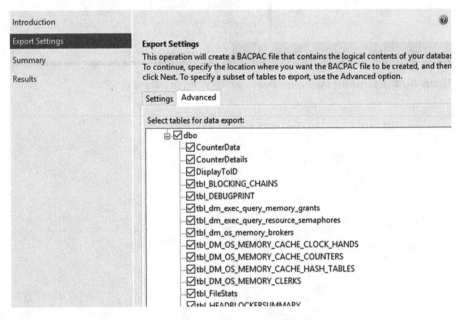

Figure 8-15. *Choosing the objects to be included in the bacpac file*

If SQL Server identifies any migration blockers during the creating of the bacpac file, those blockers are logged in the Export report at the end of the Export Data Tier operation (see Figure 8-16).

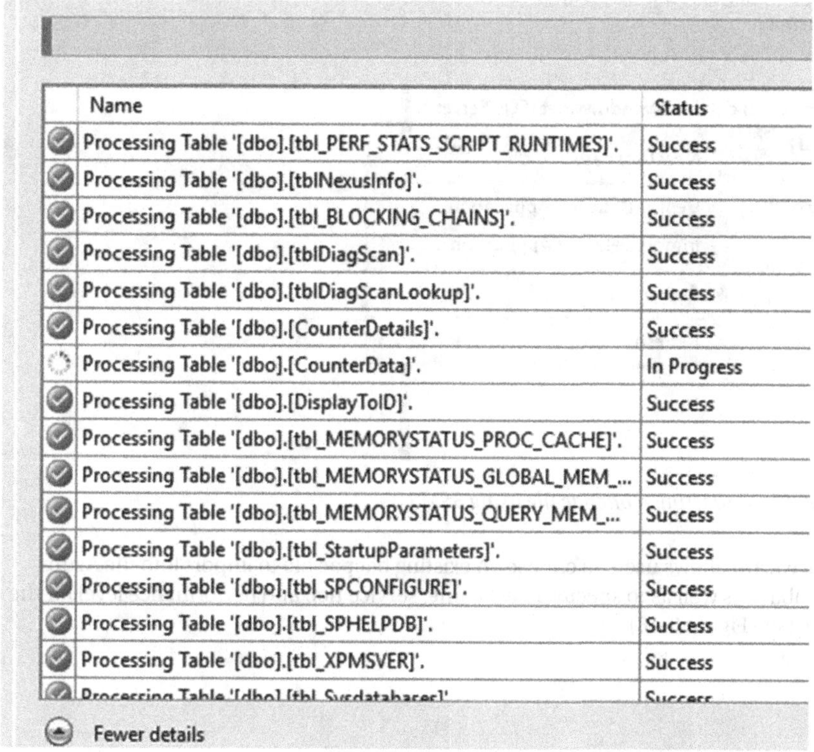

Name	Status
Processing Table '[dbo].[tbl_PERF_STATS_SCRIPT_RUNTIMES]'.	Success
Processing Table '[dbo].[tblNexusInfo]'.	Success
Processing Table '[dbo].[tbl_BLOCKING_CHAINS]'.	Success
Processing Table '[dbo].[tblDiagScan]'.	Success
Processing Table '[dbo].[tblDiagScanLookup]'.	Success
Processing Table '[dbo].[CounterDetails]'.	Success
Processing Table '[dbo].[CounterData]'.	In Progress
Processing Table '[dbo].[DisplayToID]'.	Success
Processing Table '[dbo].[tbl_MEMORYSTATUS_PROC_CACHE]'.	Success
Processing Table '[dbo].[tbl_MEMORYSTATUS_GLOBAL_MEM_...	Success
Processing Table '[dbo].[tbl_MEMORYSTATUS_QUERY_MEM_...	Success
Processing Table '[dbo].[tbl_StartupParameters]'.	Success
Processing Table '[dbo].[tbl_SPCONFIGURE]'.	Success
Processing Table '[dbo].[tbl_SPHELPDB]'.	Success
Processing Table '[dbo].[tbl_XPMSVER]'.	Success
Processing Table '[dbo].[tbl_Sysdatabases]'.	Success

Fewer details

Figure 8-16. *Export Data Tier Application execution*

If no errors are identified in the Export Data Tier Application report, the database can be migrated to an Azure SQL Database without any issues. If errors are identified, they need to resolved before the database can be migrated to an Azure SQL database.

Performing the Database Migration

The actual database migration can be done using any of the following options.

- Export/import a bacpac file.
- Use the SSMS Deploy to Azure SQL Database wizard.
- Use Transaction Replication.

Export/Import a Bacpac File

An existing database can be exported to a bacpac file using SSMS or SQLPackage.exe, as described earlier. This exported file can then be imported to an Azure SQL database using either SQLPackage.exe or the Import Data-Tier Application wizard in SSMS, as illustrated in Figure 8-17.

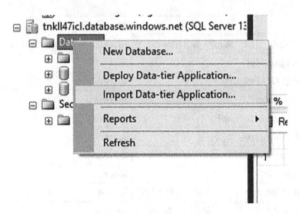

Figure 8-17. *Importing a bacpac file using SSMS*

The wizard allows users to choose an existing bacpac file to import into the Azure SQL Database as well as to specify a new name, service tier, and performance level for the database (see Figure 8-18).

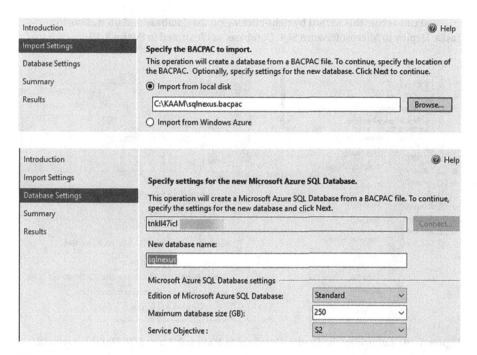

Figure 8-18. *Configuring the Azure SQL Database options during a bacpac import operation*

When you click finish, the wizard will import the contents of the bacpac file to the Azure SQL Database.

The SQLPackage.exe import action can also be used to import a bacpac file to Azure SQL Database. The command syntax would look like this:

```
sqlpackage.exe /Action:Import /SourceFile:<bacpac file to be imported>
/ssn:<AzureSQLDatabaseLogicalServer> /tdn:<DatabaseName> /tu:"AdminUserName"
/tp:<AdminUserPassword> > "OutputFile" 2>&1
```

The SSMS Deploy to Azure SQL Database Wizard

The SSMS Deploy to Azure SQL Database wizard can be used to directly migrate an existing SQL Server database to Azure SQL Database, without having to explicitly create a bacpac file and then import it. Although behind the scenes, this wizard creates temporary bacpac files which are then imported to the Azure SQL database. As with the Import Data Tier wizard mentioned earlier, users can choose which server and what service tier (and performance level) the database will be created in.

You can access this wizard by right-clicking on the database and then choosing Tasks, Deploy to Microsoft Azure SQL Database, as illustrated in Figure 8-19.

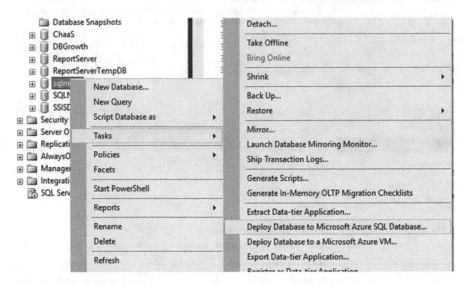

Figure 8-19. *Launching the Deploy Database to Microsoft Azure SQL Database wizard*

Figure 8-20 illustrates the different configuration options available when the database is being deployed. The wizard allows users to connect to the logical server, where the new database would be hosted, and to specify the service tier and the performance level.

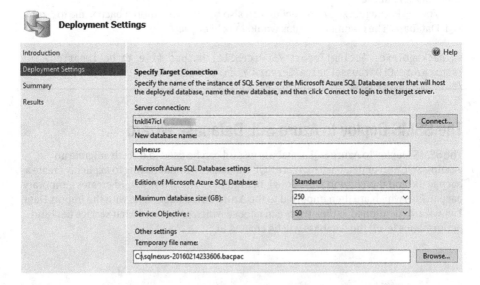

Figure 8-20. *Configuring the database options during a deploy Azure SQL database operation*

■ **Note** The migration will fail if the size of the database is larger than the maximum allowed size of the service tier.

Once the wizard completes execution, the new Azure SQL Database with the specified service tier and performance level is created on the specified logical server (see Figure 8-21).

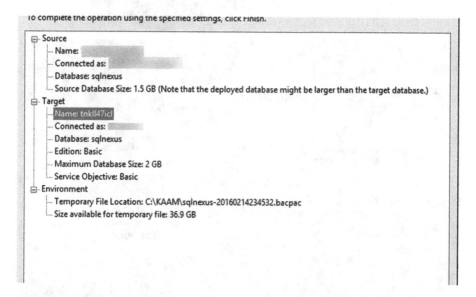

Figure 8-21. Deploy database to Microsoft Azure SQL Database wizard summary page

Using Transaction Replication

Transaction Replication is a data (or schema) replication feature of Microsoft SQL Server that replicates transactions on the source database (publisher) to the multiple target databases (subscribers), through an intermediate distribution database. The Log Reader agent reads the transaction log file from the publisher database and sends the information to the distribution database. Once the information is available with the distribution database, it is send to the subscribers using the distribution agents.

SQL Server Transaction Replication allows users to configure Azure SQL databases as a subscriber. During the initial setup of transactional replication, the subscriber database is synced using a snapshot of the publisher database. After the initial sync, any changes made to the primary database (on-premises) are captured by logRead.exe and stored in the distribution database. From the distribution database, these changes are sent to the Azure SQL database subscriber. This flow is illustrated in Figure 8-22.

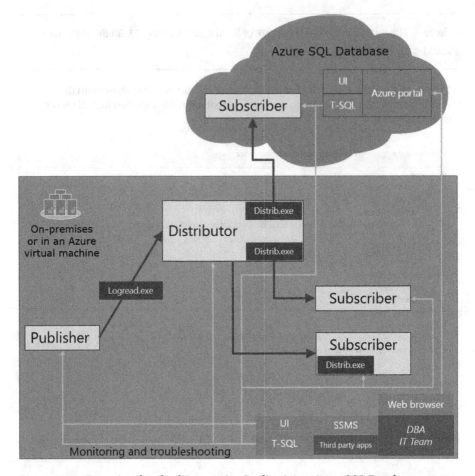

Figure 8-22. Execution details of Transaction Replication to Azure SQL Database

Azure SQL Database cannot be configured as a distributor or as a publisher for a transactional replication setup. This feature can be used as an effective option for database migration, especially in scenarios where minimal or no downtime is required.

Summary

In this chapter, we learned about the internal architecture workings of Azure SQL Database. We also looked at the different service tiers and performance levels of Azure SQL Database and how different utilities—such as the Azure Portal, SSMS, SSDT, and PowerShell—can be used to create and manage an Azure SQL database. We also learned about the different methods available to migrate an existing SQL Server database to Azure SQL Database.

CHAPTER 9

■ ■ ■

Business Continuity and Security with Azure SQL Database

Business continuity is all about ensuring that critical applications are resilient to planned or unplanned outages that might result in permanent or temporary loss of business functionality. The goal is to design and deploy the critical business so that these outages will have minimal or no impact on the business, or there is scope for recovery within a business-approved timeframe. There are several key discussion points that you need to consider when you're planning or designing for business continuity.

- *Recovery time objective (RTO)*. The maximum possible allowed downtime for the application, post which the business might incur monetary losses. Applications need to be designed such that they recover within the specified RTO.

- *Recovery point objective (RPO)*. The maximum amount of data loss allowed before the applications need to be fully available.

- *Estimated Recovery Time (ERT)*. The estimated duration for the database to be fully available after a restore or failover request.

When designing applications for business continuity, architects need to consider multiple types of planned or unplanned outages that can cause the application to fail. Some of the most common scenarios are:

- *Human errors*. Recovering from scenarios where an admin or a user with elevated privileges has deleted or modified critical business data by mistake. This is a very common scenario that folks working with SQL Server or related technologies are all too familiar with.

- *Site outages.* Recovering from scenarios where the entire data center is unavailable. Examples include natural catastrophes and electrical malfunctions that render the entire DC unavailable.

- *Maintenance and upgrades.* Ensuring business continuity during application maintenance and upgrades.

In this chapter, we will talk about the various business continuity and disaster recovery options available with Azure SQL Database and how these features can be utilized to provide a highly available database environment for your business-critical workloads.

While business continuity and disaster recovery are of paramount importance, another key criterion for any critical workload is to ensure the security and safety of the data stored on the database. We should be careful during the design and architecting phase to ensure that the final solution is secure against all potential external or internal attacks. In this chapter, we will cover the different security features and options available with the Azure SQL Database to ensure the safety of your data.

Azure SQL Database: Business Continuity and Disaster Recovery

Azure SQL Database provides out-of-the box high availability and fault tolerance, which goes a long way in ensuring business continuity and disaster recovery. Additionally, there are other configurable options that can be utilized to achieve high availability/disaster recovery across multiple regions.

Local Redundancy

Azure SQL Database by default provides two secondary copies of the database in the same data center. These secondaries are in sync with the primary copy of the database. All the read/write operations are performed on the primary copy. Additionally, the writes are replicated to the secondary copies. Figure 9-1 shows this process.

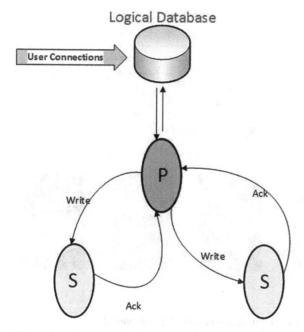

Figure 9-1. *Representational view of Azure SQL DB local redundancy*

Azure presents a transparent logical copy of the database to the end users, keeping other details hidden. If one of the copies goes down, Azure ensures that another copy of the database is created to maintain three copies of the database. Azure uses the Partition Manager and Global Partition Map to ensure that three copies of the database are maintained at any given point in time.

When a database is created, Azure creates the two secondary copies on different data nodes. As illustrated in Figure 9-2, if the node containing the primary copy of the database is down, Azure Partition Manager initiates a failover algorithm wherein one of the secondary copies is promoted to the primary role. Once the primary database copy is established, another secondary is created and synched with the primary.

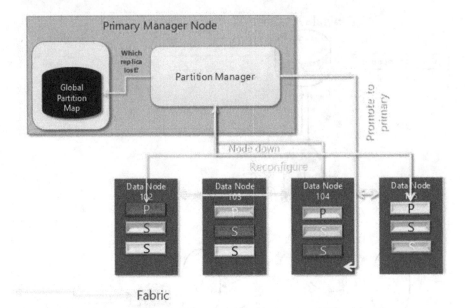

Figure 9-2. Detailed representation of how local redundancy is achieved

If the node containing a secondary copy was down, the Partition Manager creates a new secondary copy on one of the nodes in order to ensure that there are three copies. In the following example, when the node 103 goes down, all the copies of the database on that node are moved to other nodes. This process is illustrated in Figures 9-2 and 9-3.

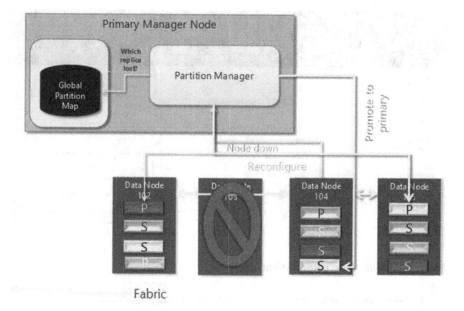

Figure 9-3. *Reconfiguring local redundancy on a node failure*

Point-in-Time Restore

Azure SQL Database service provides automatic backup capabilities for all databases. The retention of these backups is dependent on the service tier the database is running in. For example, for a database running in the basic service tier, the backups are retained for seven days, while for standard and premium service tiers, the retention is 14 days and 35 days, respectively. The database can be restored to any point in time within the retention period from the backups. These backups are stored on a geo-redundant storage account with read access to the geo-copy.

Azure SQL Database service takes full backups every week, differential backups every day, and log backup every five minutes. The first full backup is taken immediately after the database is created. Once the first full backup is completed, the other backups are scheduled automatically. Point-in-time restore can be completed using the Azure Portal or using PowerShell, as illustrated in Figure 9-4.

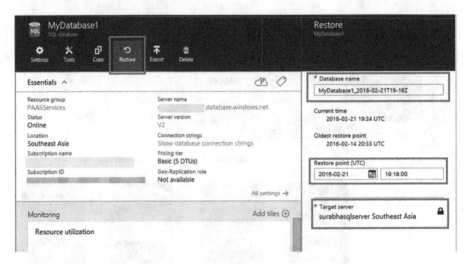

Figure 9-4. *Initiating a point-in-time restore*

Consider these few key points with regard to the restore operation:

- Restore creates a new database on the **same** logical SQL Server and with the service tier, which was the being used during the restore point. Since the database is on the same logical server, it's important to ensure that there are enough DTUs on the server for the new database.

- The time for restore is dependent on multiple factors like the size of the database, recovery point (how far back in time), the number of backups to be restored, etc.

- Once the database is restored, it would be charged fully in accordance to the service tier and performance level being used.

If a database was deleted, the final backup of the database is retained in accordance with the retention policy. A deleted database can be restored to the point at which it was deleted. The deleted databases can be viewed in the Azure Portal under the logical server where the database resided. Figure 9-5 illustrates how a deleted database can be restored using the Azure Management Portal.

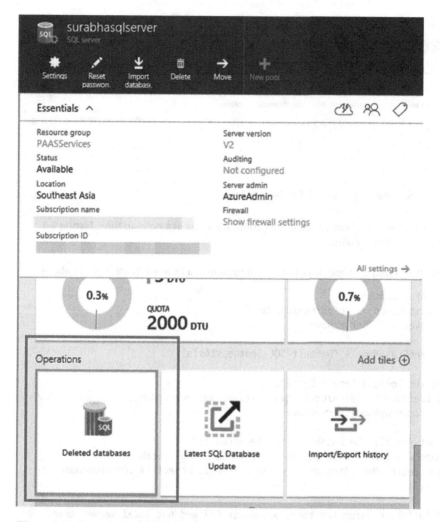

Figure 9-5. *Restoring a deleted database*

As illustrated in Figure 9-6, the deleted date and the restore point are the same, meaning that the database would be restored to the point when it was deleted.

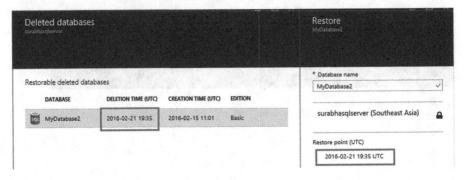

Figure 9-6. *Initiating a deleted database restore*

Azure PowerShell can be used to restore a database at a point in time. Listing 9-1 provides the sample code.

Listing 9-1. Point-in-Time Restore and Restoration of a Deleted Azure SQL Database

```
Login-AzureRmAccount
#$resourceGroup = "ResourceGroupName"
#$DbServer = "DBServerName"

$resourceGroupName = "Default-SQL-SoutheastAsia"

# Get the Logical Server Details
$DbServerName = (Get-AzureRmSqlServer -ResourceGroupName
$resourceGroupName).ServerName

#1. Get for all the Databases on the account.
$DBName = Get-AzureRmSqlDatabase -ServerName $DbServerName
-ResourceGroupName $resourceGroupName | Where-Object {$_.DatabaseName -ne
"Master"}

## PointInTime Parameter takes values in GMT and not local server time.
$RestoreRequest = Restore-AzureRmSqlDatabase -FromPointInTimeBackup
-PointInTime "2016-05-17 04:00:00" -ResourceId $DBName[0].ResourceId
-ServerName $DbServerName -TargetDatabaseName ($DBName[0].DatabaseName+"_
Restored") -ResourceGroupName $resourceGroupName
if($RestoreRequest -ne $null)
{
    Write-Host "Database Restored Successfully!!"
}

## Restore a Deleted Database
## in this example we will retrieve all the deleted databases and then
restore the first database in the list.
```

```
$deletedDBs = Get-AzureRMSqlDeletedDatabaseBackup -ResourceGroupName
$resourceGroupName -ServerName $DbServerName
$RestoredDB = Restore-AzureRmSqlDatabase -FromDeletedDatabaseBackup
-DeletionDate $deletedDBs[0].DeletionDate -ResourceId $deletedDBs[0].
ResourceId -ServerName $deletedDBs[0].ServerName -ResourceGroupName
$deletedDBs[0].ResourceGroupName -ServiceObjectiveName $deletedDBs[0].
ServiceLevelObjective -TargetDatabaseName $deletedDBs[0].DatabaseName
if($RestoredDB -ne $null)
{
    Write-Host "Database Restored Successfully!!"
}
```

Geo-Restore

The Azure SQL Database Geo-Restore capability allows for the restoration of the database from the geo-redundant copy of the backups. As mentioned previously, Azure takes automated backups of the databases on a geo-redundant storage. Geo-Restore uses these geo-replicated copies of the backup for the restore purposes. Geo-Restore can help applications recover quickly from a disaster that impacts the entire primary site.

■ **Note** There might be some delay between when the backups are taken and when they are replicated to the GRS. It is entirely possible that the last backup was not replicated before the primary site went down.

As with point-in-time restores, Geo-Restores can be done using the Azure Portal (see Figures 9-7 and 9-8) or using PowerShell (see Listing 9-2).

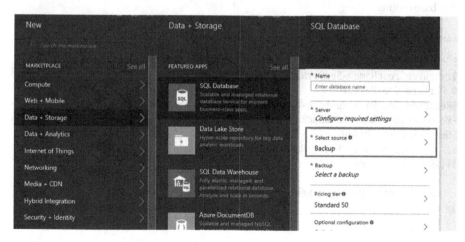

Figure 9-7. Initiating Geo-Restore

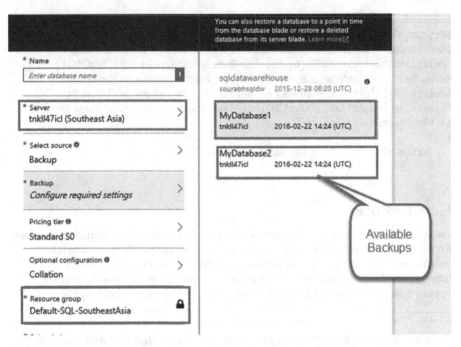

Figure 9-8. *Configuring Geo-Restore options*

Geo-Restore can be achieved by creating a new database with the source as the geo-redundant backups.

As with point-in-time restores, the time needed to restore the database depends on the size of the database being restored and the number of operations required to get the database online.

Listing 9-2. Geo-Restoring an Azure SQL Database

```
$GeoBackups = Get-AzureRMSqlDatabaseGeoBackup -ResourceGroupName
$resourceGroupName -ServerName $DbServerName
# Perform Geo-Restore
$Restored_Geo_DB = Restore-AzureRmSqlDatabase -FromGeoBackup
-ResourceGroupName $GeoBackups[0].ResourceGroupName -ResourceId
$GeoBackups[0].ResourceId -TargetDatabaseName  ($GeoBackups[0].DatabaseName
+ "_Geo_Restored") -ServerName $DbServerName
if($RestoredDB -ne $null)
{
    Write-Host "Database Restored Successfully!!"
}
```

Geo-Replication

Geo-Replication provides the ability to create geographically disparate secondary replicas of the primary databases. Geo-Replication is available in two flavors—Standard Geo-Replication, available with the Standard and the Premium service tier, and the Active Geo-Replication, available only with Premium service tier.

Unlike on-premises high availability technologies (like SQL Server AlwaysOn), Geo-Replication is always asynchronous in nature. Transactions on the primary copy are shipped to the secondary copy and applied asynchronously. To safeguard against network issues between DCs or distance based latency, the changes on the primary copy are buffered and then shipped to the secondary copy.

■ **Note**   Geo-Replication is not available with basic tier databases.

Standard Geo-Replication

Standard Geo-Replication allows for the creation of (at most) one secondary replica (non-readable) to a Microsoft designated "DR Pair" region (see Figure 9-9). The list of Microsoft designated DR pair regions can be found at:

```
http://blogs.msdn.com/b/windowsazurestorage/archive/2013/12/11/introducing-
read-access-geo-replicated-storage-ra-grs-for-windows-azure-storage.aspx
```

Figure 9-9. Representational view of the standard Geo-Replication

The secondary replica is non-readable while the primary is up and running. A manual failover is required to make the database available for user access. Standard Geo-Replication provides the classic DR scenario, wherein if the primary replica has some issue, the secondary can be immediately brought online.

Standard Geo-Replication can be set up using either the Management Portal, as illustrated in Figures 9-10 through 9-12, or by using PowerShell (see Listing 9-3).

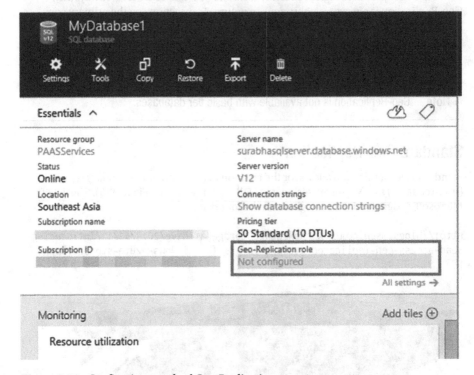

Figure 9-10. *Configuring standard Geo-Replication*

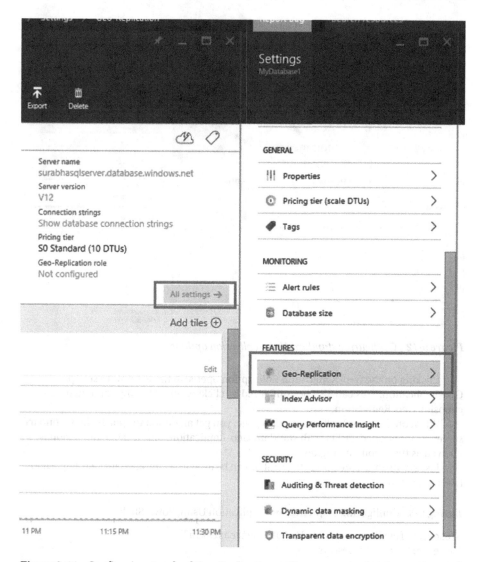

Figure 9-11. *Configuring standard Geo-Replication options*

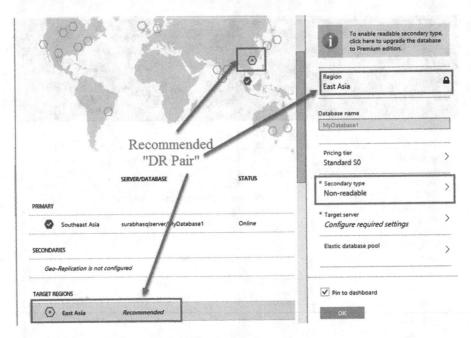

Figure 9-12. *Configuring standard Geo-Replication options*

Clicking on the Geo-Replication Role option opens up the window to set up Geo-Replication. This can also be configured by clicking on All Settings and then choosing Geo-Replication.

When on the Geo-Replication setup page, you get an option to specify the secondary server. As mentioned earlier with standard Geo-Replication, only a "DR Pair" region is allowed as the secondary region.

Just as with the Azure Portal, PowerShell can be used to set up standard Geo-Replication (see Listing 9-3).

Listing 9-3. Configuring Standard Geo-Replication Using PowerShell

```
$resourceGroupName = "Default-SQL-SoutheastAsia"
$DbServerName = "primarysvr"
$SecondaryServerName = "secondsvr"

$DBName = Get-AzureRmSqlDatabase -ServerName $DbServerName
-ResourceGroupName $resourceGroupName | Where-Object {($_.Edition -eq
"Standard") -and ($_.DatabaseName -ne "master")}

$replicationLink = New-AzureRmSqlDatabaseSecondary -DatabaseName $DBName[0].
DatabaseName -ServerName $DbServerName -ResourceGroupName $resourceGroupName
-PartnerResourceGroupName $resourceGroupName -PartnerServerName
$SecondaryServerName -AllowConnections No
```

```
if($replicationLink -ne $null)
{
    Write-Host "Standard Geo Replication Setup successfully!!"
}
```

Since the database in this case is configured with the standard tier, the only option allowed here is to have a non-readable secondary copy. This property can be verified using the Management Portal (see Figure 9-13).

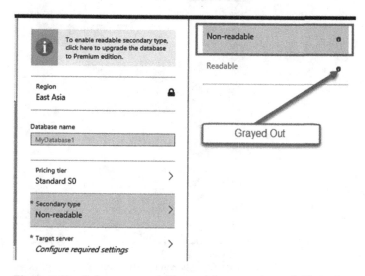

Figure 9-13. *Only a non-readable secondary copy is available in this case*

Once replication is configured, the status of the database changes accordingly. For example, as shown in Figure 9-14, the primary database would show the Geo-Replication role status as Primary, while the secondary copy would show up as Secondary.

Status	Server version
Online	V12
Location	Connection strings
Southeast Asia	Show database connection strings
Subscription name	Pricing tier
	S0 Standard (10 DTUs)
Subscription ID	Geo-Replication role
	Primary

All settings →

Resource group	Server name
PAASServices	sourabhsqlsecondary.database.windows.net
Status	Server version
Online	V12
Location	Connection strings
East Asia	Show database connection strings
Subscription name	Pricing tier
	S0 Standard (10 DTUs)
Subscription ID	Geo-Replication role
	Secondary

All settings →

Figure 9-14. *Database status has changed*

Performing Database Failover

The Azure Portal provides a very easy one-click mechanism to failover the database when the primary database is down (see Figure 9-15). You simply need to browse to the Geo-Replication settings and then click on the secondary database and initiate failover. Azure also provides a mechanism to stop replication if required.

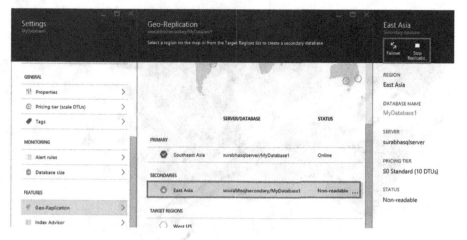

Figure 9-15. *Performing database failover*

PowerShell can also be used to failover a database to the secondary replica.

```
Set-AzureRMSqlDatabaseSecondary -DatabaseName $DBName[0].DatabaseName
-PartnerResourceGroupName $resourceGroup -ResourceGroupName $resourceGroup
-ServerName $SecondaryServer -Failover -AllowDataLoss
```

Active Geo-Replication

Active Geo-Replication uses the same technology as the standard Geo-Replication, but has the following differences (see Figure 9-16):

- The secondaries are readable.

- There can be up to four secondaries in any data center across the globe. Users can create the secondary in any data centre, irrespective of the DR Pair regions.

- Active Geo-Replication is available only for the Premium tier databases.

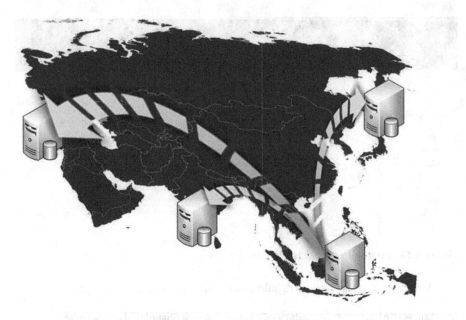

Figure 9-16. *Representation view of the Active Geo-Replication*

As with Standard Geo-Replication, Active Geo-Replication can be set using the Azure Portal, as shown in Figures 9-17 and 9-18, or by using PowerShell, as shown in Listing 9-4.

Figure 9-17. *Configuring Active Geo-Replication*

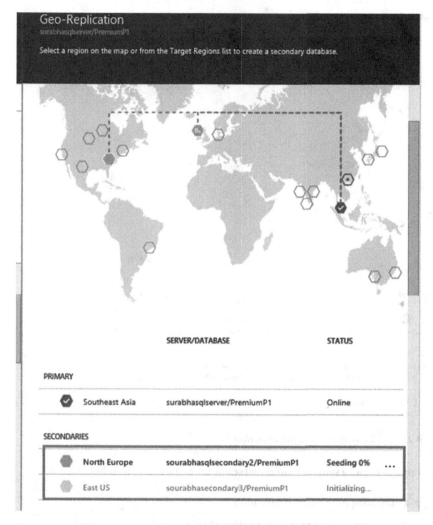

Figure 9-18. *Initialization of Active Geo-Replication*

As mentioned, with Active Geo-Replication, up to four secondaries can be created (each in a different region). All the secondaries are readable and can be utilized for read-only workloads (such as running reports). If there is a problem with the primary server, a manual failover can be initiated to recover the secondary database and make it available for the application workload. Figure 9-18 represents a scenario with two Active Geo-Replication secondaries.

Database failover can be performed using Azure Portal or PowerShell. After the failover, the new primary database goes into the "Online" state, while the new secondary goes into the "Readable" state. As can be seen in Figure 9-19, the East US database is now the primary database, while the Southeast Asia database has become a readable secondary database.

Figure 9-19. *Active Geo-Replication in Action*

Listing 9-4 shows a sample PowerShell script to enable Active Geo-Replication.

Listing 9-4. Enabling Active Geo-Replication

```
$resourceGroupName = "Default-SQL-SoutheastAsia"
$DbServerName = "primarysvr"
$SecondaryServerName = "secondsvr"

$DBName = Get-AzureRmSqlDatabase -ServerName $DbServerName
-ResourceGroupName $resourceGroupName | Where-Object {($_.Edition -eq
"Premium") -and ($_.DatabaseName -ne "master")}
$replicationLink = New-AzureRmSqlDatabaseSecondary -DatabaseName $DBName[0].
DatabaseName -ServerName $DbServerName -ResourceGroupName $resourceGroupName
-PartnerResourceGroupName $resourceGroupName -PartnerServerName
$SecondaryServerName -AllowConnections All
```

```
if($replicationLink -ne $null)
{
    Write-Host "Geo Replication Setup successfully!!"
}
```

The "Allow Connections" Parameter to the New-AzureRmSqlDatabaseSecondary cmdlet is of paramount importance. If the "All" option is not specified, Azure will end up creating a non-readable secondary copy of the database.

SQL Server Replication

SQL Server Transactional Replication (and Snapshot Replication) can be set up between an on-premises SQL Server or a SQL Server running on Azure VM to an Azure SQL database. The following key considerations must be made while setting up replication between SQL Server publisher and Azure SQL Database subscriber (see Figure 9-20).

- The publisher and distributor can be an on-premises SQL Server instance or a SQL Server running on Azure VM. The minimum supported build for SQL Server is SQL Server 2012 SP2 CU8.

- The subscriber (Azure SQL Database) should be in a push subscription, meaning the distribution agent will run on the distribution server.

- All replication monitoring and management needs to be performed from the publisher server.

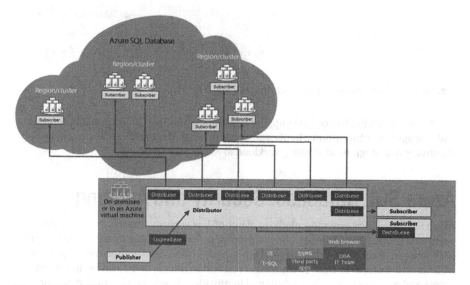

Figure 9-20. *SQL replication to Azure SQL Database*

Replication to Azure SQL Database can be set up using either SQL Server Management Studio, as illustrated in Figure 9-21, or using T-SQL scripts. When you're selecting the subscription for an existing publication or a new publication, the Azure SQL Database server and the database can be specified.

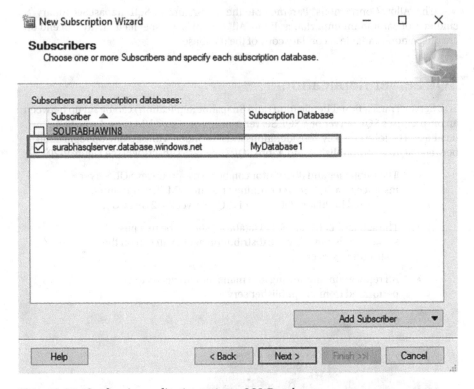

Figure 9-21. *Configuring replication to Azure SQL Database*

Once replication has been set up, the Replication Monitor can be used to monitor and manage the subscriptions. Replication to Azure SQL Database can be used in an effective way to migrate an existing workload to Azure SQL Database.

Azure SQL Database: Security and Auditing

Azure SQL databases provide a plethora of out-of-box security features to ensure that users data residing on Azure are not compromised at any cost. The multi-layered security available with Azure SQL Database—which includes role-based authorization (just like SQL Server), features to encrypt the data at rest and in transit, data masking to restrict access and row-level security—is designed to provide full protection from any real or perceived threats.

Some of the key security features available with Azure SQL Database are covered next.

Firewall Administration

The first layer of security is provided by the Azure SQL Database firewall, which blocks all unauthorized connections to the Azure SQL Database (see Figure 9-22). Azure Portal (or PowerShell) can be used to configure the IP address (or address range) from which connections can be allowed to the Azure SQL databases (or the logical server). Connections from any other IP would be automatically refused.

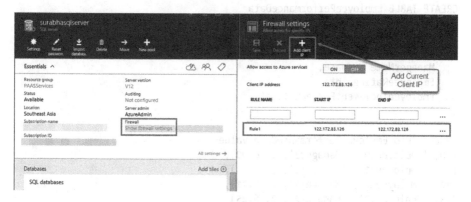

Figure 9-22. *Configuring firewall exceptions for Azure SQL databases*

Authentication and Authorization

Azure SQL Database now allows both SQL authentication and Azure Active Directory authentication (provided there is an Azure AD configured to use). Like Microsoft SQL Server, Azure SQL Database also uses role-based access authorizations. SQL Database provides both server level roles and database level roles that can be managed using the Azure Portal, PowerShell, or using SQL Server Management Studio (only database roles). Server roles and/or database roles are effective tools that can help control which user has access to what data. In addition to providing role-based access, Azure SQL Database also provides some really cool features that have not yet made it to the box SQL Server (some of these features are slated to be included in SQL Server 2016 release).

Row-Level Security

Row-Level Security (RLS) provides a way to control access to individual rows in a table. This access control is implemented using security predicates (or security functions) created in the databases. Since the access control logic (the security predicates) is available in the database, it provides a very reliable and robust security mechanism. Moreover, since the logic is implemented within the database, the access will be controlled irrespective of which application or connection is requesting data.

Listing 9-5 shows a script for implementing RLS.

Listing 9-5. T-SQL Sample Script for Implementing RLS

```
CREATE USER GeneralManager WITHOUT LOGIN;
CREATE USER Manager1 WITHOUT LOGIN;
CREATE USER Manager2 WITHOUT LOGIN;

CREATE TABLE EmployeePerformanceData
    (
    EmployeeID int,
        EmployeeName varchar(200),
    ManagerName sysname,
    EmployeeRating int,
    EmployeeIncrementPercent float
    );

INSERT into EmployeePerformanceData values
(10, 'Employee10', 'Manager2', 1,10.00),
(11, 'Employee11', 'Manager2', 3, 6.53),
(12, 'Employee12', 'Manager1', 2, 8.71),
(13, 'Employee13', 'Manager2', 3, 6.25),
(14, 'Employee14', 'Manager1', 3, 5.87),
(15, 'Employee15', 'Manager2', 5, 0.00);

SELECT * FROM EmployeePerformanceData;

GRANT SELECT ON EmployeePerformanceData TO GeneralManager;
GRANT SELECT ON EmployeePerformanceData TO Manager1;
GRANT SELECT ON EmployeePerformanceData TO Manager2;

-- If any of the users select data from the table at this point, they would
see all 6 records
EXECUTE AS USER = 'GeneralManager';
SELECT * FROM EmployeePerformanceData;
REVERT;

EXECUTE AS USER = 'Manager1';
SELECT * FROM EmployeePerformanceData;
REVERT;

EXECUTE AS USER = 'Manager2';
SELECT * FROM EmployeePerformanceData;
REVERT;

--- Implement RLS using Security Predicates and Filters
/*
```

In this case we are creating a security predicate such that the managers can only their own Employee Data and the GM can see all the employee information.
```
*/
CREATE SCHEMA Security;
GO

CREATE FUNCTION Security.fn_securitypredicate(@ManagerName AS sysname)
    RETURNS TABLE
WITH SCHEMABINDING
AS
    RETURN SELECT 1 AS fn_securitypredicate_result
WHERE @ManagerName = USER_NAME() OR USER_NAME() = 'GeneralManager';

-- Tie the Security Predicate with the User Table
CREATE SECURITY POLICY SalesFilter
ADD FILTER PREDICATE Security.fn_securitypredicate(ManagerName)
ON dbo.EmployeePerformanceData
WITH (STATE = ON);

-- Now if we execute the Queries, each manager would only see their own
employee information.

EXECUTE AS USER = 'GeneralManager';
SELECT * FROM EmployeePerformanceData;
REVERT;

EXECUTE AS USER = 'Manager1';
SELECT * FROM EmployeePerformanceData;
REVERT;

EXECUTE AS USER = 'Manager2';
SELECT * FROM EmployeePerformanceData;
REVERT;

-- Disable the security Policy
ALTER SECURITY POLICY SalesFilter
WITH (STATE = OFF);
```

Dynamic Data Masking

Data masking prevents exposure or unauthorized access to sensitive data by masking the database before it's presented to the users. Data masking is configured by defining security policies within the table/object definition and using the mask/unmask permissions to control whether a user sees masked or unmasked data. Database owners and admins always see unmasked data.

A sample script to test data masking is included in Listing 9-6.

Listing 9-6. T-SQL Sample Script for Implementing Data Masking

```
CREATE TABLE Employee
(
EmployeeID int IDENTITY PRIMARY KEY,
FirstName varchar(100) MASKED WITH (FUNCTION = 'partial(1,"XXXXXXX",0)')
NULL,
LastName varchar(100) NOT NULL,
Phone# varchar(12) MASKED WITH (FUNCTION = 'default()') NULL,
Email varchar(100) MASKED WITH (FUNCTION = 'email()') NULL,
Salary float Masked with (Function='random(1,7)') Null
);

INSERT Employee (FirstName, LastName, Phone#, Email, Salary) VALUES
('Roberto', 'Tamburello', '555.123.4567', 'RTamburello@contoso.
com',100000.00),
('Janice', 'Galvin', '555.123.4568', 'JGalvin@contoso.com.co',200000.00),
('Zheng', 'Mu', '555.123.4569', 'ZMu@contoso.net',100000.00),
('Bill', 'Anderson', '555.123.4570', 'billand@contoso.net',150000.00),
('Graham', 'Scott', '555.123.4571', 'Grahamsco@contoso.net',120000.00);

SELECT * FROM Employee;

CREATE USER AppUser WITHOUT LOGIN;
GRANT SELECT ON Employee TO AppUser;

EXECUTE AS USER = 'AppUser';
SELECT * FROM Employee;
REVERT;
```

The user AppUser will see the following output (see Figure 9-23) with all sensitive information masked. The DBO, on the other hand, will see all the data as is.

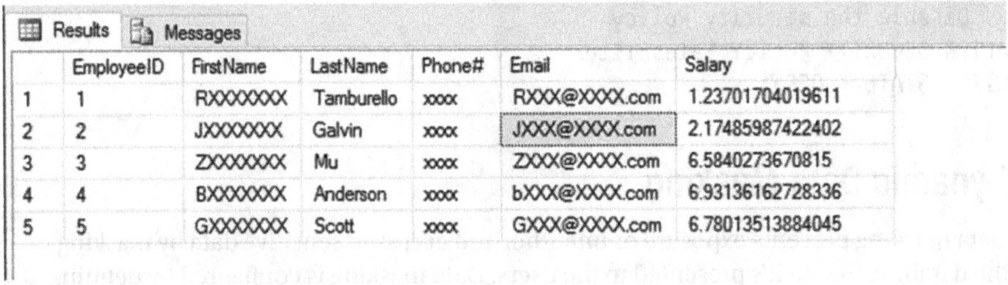

	EmployeeID	FirstName	LastName	Phone#	Email	Salary
1	1	RXXXXXXX	Tamburello	xxxx	RXXX@XXXX.com	1.23701704019611
2	2	JXXXXXXX	Galvin	xxxx	JXXX@XXXX.com	2.17485987422402
3	3	ZXXXXXXX	Mu	xxxx	ZXXX@XXXX.com	6.5840273670815
4	4	BXXXXXXX	Anderson	xxxx	bXXX@XXXX.com	6.93136162728336
5	5	GXXXXXXX	Scott	xxxx	GXXX@XXXX.com	6.78013513884045

Figure 9-23. *Data masking*

SQL Database Auditing

SQL Database Auditing provides the ability to track key events on the databases and store them on Azure Storage. These audit logs can then be utilized for regulatory compliance requirements or to provide a benchmark (or analysis) of the activities on the database. Auditing is available in all service tiers.

Additionally, auditing can be configured at a logical server level (which will ensure all DBs on the server are being audited) or at a database level (see Figure 9-24). Auditing can be configured using Azure Portal or PowerShell.

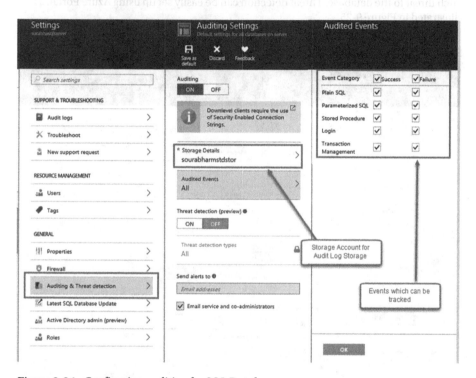

Figure 9-24. *Configuring auditing for SQL Database*

■ **Note** After SQL Database Auditing is enabled, you might need to change your connection string to the SQL database from downstream clients, or your applications will fail to connect to the database. For example, replication to SQL database will fail after enabling auditing, since the distributor agent will fail to connect to the subscriber. In such cases, make sure to use the connection string `<server name>.database.secure.windows.net`.

Auditing data is available for consumption in a dashboard format in Azure Portal or can be exported to Excel and analyzed there.

SQL Database Threat Detection

SQL Database Threat Detection provides a mechanism to detect and respond to potential threats (anomalous activities) to the SQL database. Using a combination of threat detection and auditing, users can investigate and then take necessary actions on any such threat to the database. Threat detection can be easily set up using Azure Portal, as illustrated in Figure 9-25.

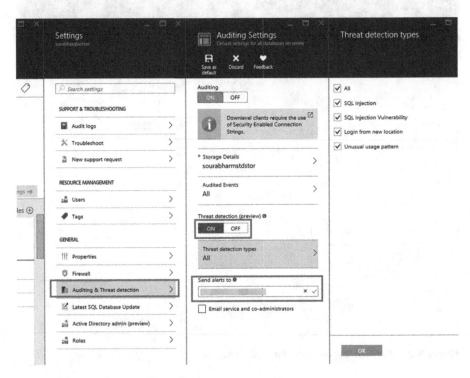

Figure 9-25. *Configuring threat detection*

Encryption

Azure SQL Database provides a plethora of encryption features to ensure that data residing on the database is not compromised. These features provide protection to data both at rest and in transit, discussed next.

Connection Encryption

Azure SQL Database allows users to use an encrypted SSL connection to the database. To ensure that the connection to SQL Database is encrypted, application developers need to use the "Encrypt = True" connection string parameter.

Transparent Data Encryption

Transparent Data Encryption (TDE) is not a new feature and has been around since SQL Server 2008. It provides a way to encrypt the data at rest. Azure SQL databases use the same technology to provide a way to encrypt all data at rest. Transparent Data Encryption can be enabled by using either the Azure Portal (or PowerShell) or the following T-SQL code.

```
Alter Database [MyDatabase1] set Encryption On
```

The PowerShell cmdlet Get-AzureRMSqlDatabaseTransparentDataEncryption can also be used to set TDE on the SQL database.

Cell-Level (or Column Data) Encryption

Column data encryption is not a new feature and users familiar with SQL Server know that this can be achieved by using a combination of symmetric keys and the EncryptByKey (or DecryptByKey) functions available with SQL. The key is to use the EncryptByKey function along with the key during data insert or update and the DecryptByKey function for SELECT operations.

The T-SQL script in Listing 9-7 creates a table to store encrypted data.

Listing 9-7. Sample T-SQL Script for Storing Encrypted Data

```
IF NOT EXISTS (SELECT * FROM sys.symmetric_keys WHERE symmetric_key_id = 101)
    CREATE MASTER KEY ENCRYPTION BY
    PASSWORD = 'ThisisaveryveryStr0ngPAss@w0rd1'
GO


CREATE CERTIFICATE EncryptCert
    WITH SUBJECT = 'Some Random Subject';
GO
```

```
CREATE SYMMETRIC KEY SymmetricKey
    WITH ALGORITHM = AES_256
    ENCRYPTION BY CERTIFICATE EncryptCert;
GO

-- Create a column in which to store the encrypted data.
Create table CustomerInfo
(
CustomerID int Identity Primary Key,
CustomerName varchar(200),
CustomerPhone varbinary(100),
CustomerEmail varbinary(200),
CustomerCreditCard varbinary(200)
)

-- Open the symmetric key with which to encrypt the data.
Begin Tran
OPEN SYMMETRIC KEY SymmetricKey
    DECRYPTION BY CERTIFICATE EncryptCert;
insert into CustomerInfo (CustomerName,CustomerPhone,CustomerEmail,Customer
CreditCard) values
(
'Mike Anderson',
EncryptByKey(Key_GUID('SymmetricKey'),'555-123-1234'),
EncryptByKey(Key_GUID('SymmetricKey'),'mikeand@contoso.com'),
EncryptByKey(Key_GUID('SymmetricKey'),'1234567891011123')
)
Commit

-- Decrypt the Data
Begin Tran
OPEN SYMMETRIC KEY SymmetricKey
    DECRYPTION BY CERTIFICATE EncryptCert;

Select CustomerId,CustomerName,
convert(varchar,DecryptbyKey(CustomerPhone)) as Phone,
convert(varchar,DecryptbyKey(CustomerEmail)) as Email,
convert(varchar,DecryptbyKey(CustomerCreditCard)) as CreditCard
From CustomerInfo
Commit
```

Always Encrypted

Always Encrypted is a new feature available with Azure SQL Database and SQL Server 2016, and it allows clients to manage encryption of sensitive data within the application, never having to expose the information to the database layer. Since the encryption logic is not exposed to the database layers, database admins and server admins do not have access or control over the actual sensitive information.

Always Encrypted supports both Deterministic Encryption and Random Encryption. *Deterministic Encryption* will always generate the same encrypted output for the same plan text, while *Random Encryption* generates a different value every time. Deterministic Encryption, while useful in scenarios where the encrypted data needs to be searched or joined, can be more susceptible to attacks.

AlwaysOn uses two different keys—the Column Master key and the Column Encryption key, which is encrypted using the Column Master key. Listing 9-8 implements Always Encrypted on an Azure SQL database.

Listing 9-8. Sample T-SQL Script for Implementing Always Encrypted

```
USE [MyDatabase1]
GO

CREATE COLUMN MASTER KEY [CMKey]
WITH
(
        KEY_STORE_PROVIDER_NAME = N'AZURE_KEY_VAULT',
        KEY_PATH = N'https://<KeyVaultName>.vault.azure.net/keys/
AlwaysEncryptedkey'
)
GO

CREATE COLUMN ENCRYPTION KEY [CEKey]
WITH VALUES
(
        COLUMN_MASTER_KEY = [CMKey],
        ALGORITHM = 'RSA_OAEP',
        ENCRYPTED_VALUE =
0x016E000001630075007200720065006E0074007500730065007200 2F006D0079002F0034
00660033006500370066006400370036003100310033003600340034006100360031006300
0310033006400660039003700300006200320033006200370061003200620063006600390
06600380066000DEF701B5FAB3F23266DADCAAE7B448122BA75BF1841DEF7143A45C16D
37AA4AC57799D50596BA92C0406CC30A3D755D6F5D260DCCA42BB9926136985A7CCF4537
B85330DA7C1B12047048A51B04A352F6C3E71BEFEAE777019506D11AC71AF8A7AEC4DE7F
5B98ACF6EF7D56B0706E0D521533514335E500E476C6B1777212CE043BDD09B20BB97B5C7
31CB4D58BF8DDA38A7DF08EECE797DCC15A9E25B064003DE869F6D87B75A3F6625A0162
92C3B8D8F8D3876DE62DDEE57F7BC2C901E3A2097B8E050862BEA0E33EF434D2DED6D5F2
E54745D6E5C616932C5F2144B623C48B7643EDECE4CA545C31AB23DD2DFDF8067D25C05E
F1786CCBC110E005D1567B53D6E34ACCC02052F6E9AE7365DE30856EF9DB5EC4315770
D255FA76A9865204E8FBE5419AB5836480DE8345141073EB113E012CBF7132DCC22
A3A32B6E44B961DDE2B0E7F24733062412CEF9C1A0DC96976A97D48EE5DCE4F5AE12
13E680A31ADDFD9344A004ED59C6168CB7D5C8E42A22676A7D64F59A4C1687C61B5F603
49699A45D11B8EE7DC8DBB61A156AE70449483D93073497B23597A5F340A98FB7BD37D9
DC926360E32F927BB672F6BE1FFC5C01760827AF24B603E184479905BA5DFA9C23E523
182F7C5C8ABC53E5D6E6CB3806C5707EDBB7CAC3DE50DA4A2FC38D27EE65F2638FFF
37483ABC1050EEAD835919B384BB9136C0F24A6BD9489910
)
GO
```

```
CREATE TABLE dbo.EncryptedTable
(
  ID INT IDENTITY(1,1) PRIMARY KEY,

  LastName NVARCHAR(32) COLLATE Latin1_General_BIN2
    ENCRYPTED WITH
    (
        ENCRYPTION_TYPE = DETERMINISTIC,
        ALGORITHM = 'AEAD_AES_256_CBC_HMAC_SHA_256',
        COLUMN_ENCRYPTION_KEY = [CEKey]
    ) NOT NULL,

  Salary INT
    ENCRYPTED WITH
    (
        ENCRYPTION_TYPE = RANDOMIZED,
        ALGORITHM = 'AEAD_AES_256_CBC_HMAC_SHA_256',
        COLUMN_ENCRYPTION_KEY = [CEKey]
    ) NOT NULL
);
GO
```

Always Encrypted ensures that data is never in plain text, be it at rest in the database storage, or in transit from the client to database or from the database to the client.

Apart from having a plethora of features to ensure safety of data, Azure SQL Database is also complaint with various industry standards.

Summary

In this chapter, you learned about the various business continuity options available with Azure SQL Database. Geo-Replication and its associated database failover capabilities provide very robust, out-of-box disaster recovery and high availability options, and can also be used to offload some of the read workloads to the secondary database to optimize the overall database performance.

You also learned about the numerous security features available with Azure SQL Database that can be configured or utilized to ensure that your data is never compromised. With Always Encrypted, Azure SQL Database ensures that in-transit data will never be compromised, while RLS and data masking ensure that users will only see the data they are authorized to see.

CHAPTER 10

■ ■ ■

Azure SQL Database: Performance and Monitoring

Microsoft Azure SQL Database can be provisioned in different service tiers—Basic, Standard, and Premium—each with multiple performance levels—Basic, S1, S2, P1, P2, etc. Each performance level provides an increasing set of resources, which are designed to deliver increasingly higher transaction throughput.

The resources and transactional power in each service tier and performance level are expressed in terms of Database Throughput Units (DTUs). DTUs provide a way to describe the relative transaction processing capacity of a performance level based on a mix of CPU, memory, or IO rates. In essence, when migration from the S0 to S1 performance level of the standard tier (i.e., increasing the DTUs from 10 to 20) equates to doubling the processing power of the database.

In this chapter, we will explain what a DTU is and why choosing the right performance level is very important. We will also look at the various performance optimization and performance monitoring features available in Microsoft Azure SQL Database.

What Is a DTU?

A DTU is a logical representation to create a liaison between a specific and defined workload and the Azure SQL DB SKU/Performance levels. As mentioned in Chapter 8, in a very simplified description, one DTU equates to the resources required to achieve a transactional rate of ~1 transaction/sec on the database. Measuring performance in terms of DTUs provides a way to guarantee predictable performance for Azure SQL databases. For example, a database running with performance level P1 (125 DTUs) will provide a predictable transaction throughput of ~125 transactions/second.

Choosing a Performance Level

When architecting/designing for on-premises (or Azure VM) deployments of SQL Server, users have traditionally used the machine hardware specs to determine the power available to their database workloads. However, this approach doesn't work in the platform as a service world, where the hardware details are abstracted.

On-premises deployments are constrained by the fact that a lot of deliberation and calculations need to be put in before choosing the hardware specs, since scaling up the deployment might require fresh hardware investments.

Choosing the correct performance level in Azure SQL Database environment boils down to understanding the transaction throughput requirements for the database and then choosing the appropriate performance level for the database. If the chosen performance level does not meet the requirements, it's very easy to scale up (or down) the database to a different performance level, which provides a higher (or lower) throughput. Microsoft has published performance benchmarks for the different performance levels, whereby the throughput of each performance level has been summarized in terms of transaction rates per hour, per minute, and per second. The performance benchmark numbers and their summarizations can be used to determine the approximate performance levels required for the database.

Changing the Performance Level

As mentioned earlier, SQL Database service tiers or performance levels can be changed very easily using either the Azure Portal or PowerShell. This ability to change performance levels comes in handy when the user has chosen an incorrect service tier or performance level to start with or when there is a need to reduce/increase the performance level because the business is expecting a decrease/increase in the database operations.

Changing service tiers is an online operation, which means the database remains online while the change is taking effect.

PowerShell to Change the Service Tier or Performance Level

PowerShell can be utilized to configure the service tier or performance Level for a SQL database. Listing 10-1 changes the service tier of an existing database to Standard Edition, S0 performance level.

Listing 10-1. PowerShell Script to Change the Service Tier and Performance Level for an Azure SQL Database

```
#login into the Azure Account
Add-AzureRmAccount

#Select the Subscription
$subscriptions = Get-AzureRmSubscription
$SubscriptionId = $subscriptions[0].SubscriptionId
Select-AzureRmSubscription -SubscriptionId $SubscriptionId

#Select the Resource Group
$ResourceGroupName = Get-AzureRmResourceGroup | Where-Object
{$_.ResourceGroupName -notlike "Default*"}
$ResourceGroup= $ResourceGroupName[1].ResourceGroupName
```

```
#Select the Azure SQL Server and Database Name
$ServerName = (Get-AzureRmSqlServer -ResourceGroupName $ResourceGroup)[1].
ServerName
$DatabaseName = (Get-AzureRmSqlDatabase -ServerName $ServerName
-ResourceGroupName $ResourceGroup | Where-Object {$_.DatabaseName -ne
"Master"}).DatabaseName

#select the new Service Tier and Performance Level
$NewEdition = "Standard"
$NewPerformanceLevel = "S0"

# Change the Service Tier/Performance Level
$ScaleRequest = Set-AzureRmSqlDatabase -DatabaseName $DatabaseName
-ServerName $ServerName -ResourceGroupName $ResourceGroup -Edition
$NewEdition -RequestedServiceObjectiveName $NewPerformanceLevel
```

Using Azure Portal to Change the Service Tier or Performance Level

Azure Management Portal provides a single-click mechanism to change the service tiers or performance levels for your database. Figures 10-1 and 10-2 show how the service tier and the performance level of an Azure SQL Database can be changed using the Azure Management Portal.

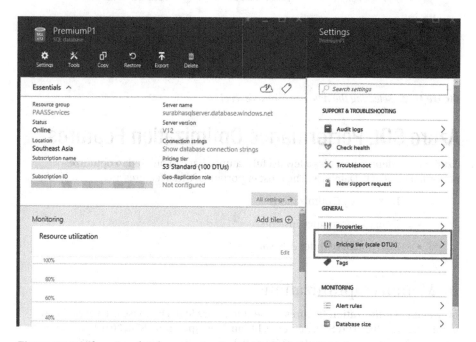

Figure 10-1. Changing database service tiers using the Azure Portal

Figure 10-2. Selecting the new performance level

Azure SQL Performance Optimization Features

Azure SQL Database provides a few useful features that can be used to optimize performance of SQL Database. The most important of these features are:

- In-Memory Optimizations
- Query Performance Insights
- SQL Database Index Advisor

In-Memory Optimizations

In-Memory Optimization features present in Azure SQL Database are very similar to the ones in Microsoft SQL Server 2014 (and the upcoming SQL 2016). In-memory optimization (in-memory tables and natively compiled SPs) and ColumnStore indexes can be used to increase the performance of both OLTP and analytics workloads. Moreover, the combination of the two can be used to provides near real-time analytics.

SQL Database Index Advisor

Azure SQL Database Index Advisor provides recommendations for indexes to be created (only non-clustered indexes) or dropped (only duplicate indexes at the time of writing) on the SQL Database. Index Advisor can be configured to automatically apply the index recommendations to the database. If the recommendations do not help performance, they can be easily rolled back. Automating index recommendations requires that query store be enabled on the Azure SQL Database.

Index recommendations can be accessed on the Azure Portal, as shown in Figure 10-3.

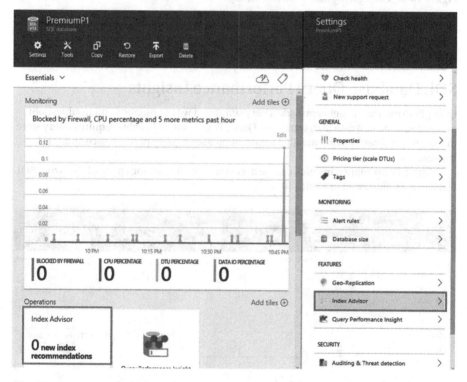

Figure 10-3. *Access the Index Advisor on Azure Portal*

To get index recommendations, a database needs a substantial amount of consistent usage and activity. Index Advisor provides better recommendations when there is consistent activity rather than inconsistent one-time burst activities. As shown in Figure 10-4, advisor settings can be configured to automatically create or drop the indexes suggested. Note that this would be an online operation and may impact queries running against the database.

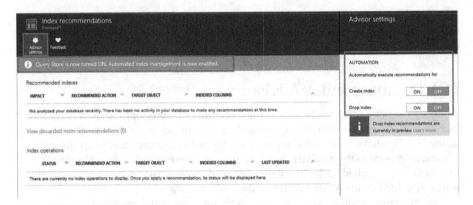

Figure 10-4. Configuring Index Advisor settings

If there are index recommendations available, they will be displayed on the page. If there are none, the advisor provides a reason as to why that's so. For example, in Figure 10-4, the reason for not having any recommendations is the absence of activity on the database.

SQL Database Query Performance Insights

Query Performance Insights provide a very simplified way to monitor and troubleshoot performance of an Azure SQL Database. Query Performance Insights requires query store to function and can provide detailed information about query performance and DTU consumption.

Query Performance Insights can be accessed from the Settings page of the Azure SQL Database, as illustrated in Figure 10-5.

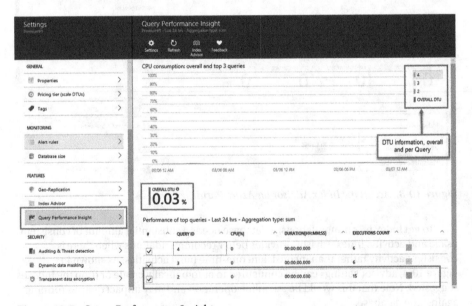

Figure 10-5. Query Performance Insights

Query Performance Insights can be used to determine the overall DTU utilization and the utilization per query. Execution details of each query can be accessed from the portal. For example, as illustrated in Figure 10-6, you can see the query text and the corresponding CPU and DTU usage by the query. Query Performance Insights settings can be tweaked to display statistics for different time periods and for different number of queries, as illustrated in Figure 10-7.

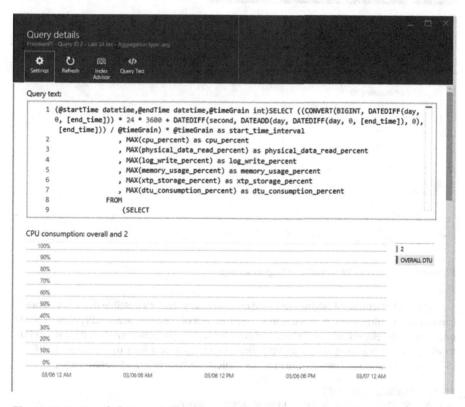

Figure 10-6. Detailed Query Performance details

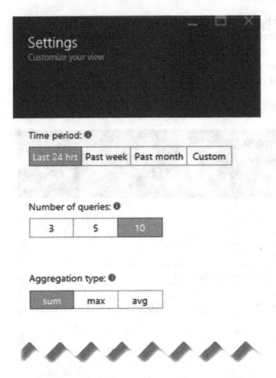

Figure 10-7. *Query Performance Insights settings*

Query Performance Insights are based on query store, and it's possible that query store can run out of storage space. When query store runs out of storage space, it will go into a read-only mode, thereby not allowing storage of any more query performance data. It is important to set up correct retention and clean-up policies for query store. Clean-up can be set to AUTO (SQL will run cleanup whenever the max size limit is reached) or a time-based retention.

```
ALTER DATABASE [YourDB]
SET QUERY_STORE (SIZE_BASED_CLEANUP_MODE = AUTO);

ALTER DATABASE [YourDB]
SET QUERY_STORE (CLEANUP_POLICY = (STALE_QUERY_THRESHOLD_DAYS = 30));
```

Query Performance Insights provides a great method to figure out problematic queries and optimize them. For example, you can get the top CPU consuming queries and tune them before they have any major performance impacts on the database.

Monitoring SQL Database

Azure provides multiple ways to monitor performance, resource utilization, and security for the SQL databases. This can be done using either Azure Portal or using DMVs (Dynamic Management View) exposed at both the database and logical server level or by using extended events configurable on the SQL database.

Using Azure Portal

Azure Portal provides a very convenient way to monitor resource utilization for SQL Database. Counters like CPU percentage, DTU percentage, and so on, can be monitored from the Azure Portal. This information can be utilized to ensure optimal health of the database. The monitoring tab on the Azure Portal (under the database details) can be utilized to monitor the resource utilization for a database (see Figure 10-8). Also, the metrics and the time period settings can be configured using the Management Portal, as per the requirements (see Figure 10-9).

Figure 10-8. *Monitoring SQL Database resource utilization*

The monitoring graphs can be edited to add multiple other counters, as shown in Figure 10-9.

Figure 10-9. *Configuring monitoring metrics*

Once the metrics have been configured, the resource utilization can be monitored on the Azure Portal, as illustrated in Figure 10-10.

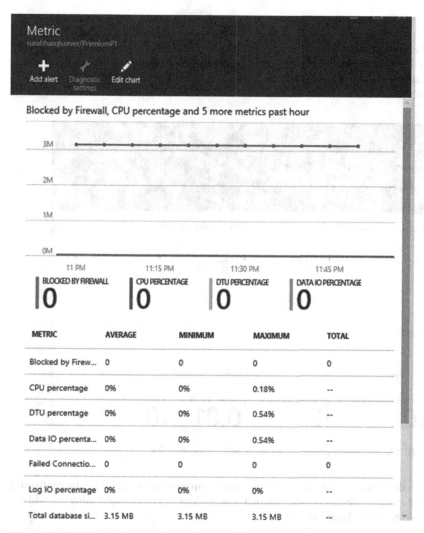

Figure 10-10. *Monitoring metrics on the portal*

Azure Portal also allows users to configure alerts against any of the available metrics (see Figure 10-11). For example, you can set up an e-mail based alert to indicate if the database crosses 80% of the maximum allowed size for the performance level, or if the DTU utilization percentage crosses 80% of the DTUs for that service tier. This information can be used to determine if the database performance level needs to be changed.

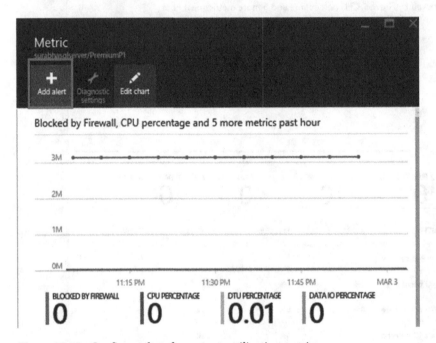

Figure 10-11. *Configure alerts for resource utilization metrics*

The alerts can be configured with the desired threshold values and can be configured to send e-mails to admins or other users. These settings can be changed using the Add an Alert Rule page (see Figure 10-12).

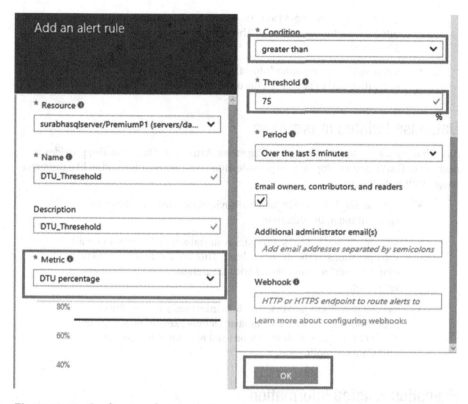

Figure 10-12. *Configuring alert properties*

Using DMV and Catalog Views

DMVs and catalog views exposed for both the database and logical servers can be used to report and/or monitor the performance, resource utilization, database object details, query execution information, and so on, of a SQL database and the logical server.

Running queries against the catalog view and DMVs requires View Server State and View Database State permissions. Some of the most commonly used DMVs are mentioned next.

Resource Utilization

Detailed information about the resource utilization (both at the logical server level and the database level) can also be obtained using the catalog views available with Azure SQL Database.

- Sys.resource_stats. Provides resource utilization information at the logical server level. The information is collected every five minutes for all the databases running on the logical server.

- `sys.dm_db_resource_stats`. Provides resource utilization information for the database. This information is collected every 15 seconds.

- `sys.event_log`. Provides information about connectivity, throttling, and deadlock events on the databases.

Database Related Information

As with resource related DMVs and catalog views, Azure SQL Database also provides a number of DMVs and catalog view to provide database-related information like the space usage, wait statistics, etc.

- `sys.dm_db_file_space_usage`. Provides information about the space usage in the database.

- `sys.dm_db_wait_stats`. Provides wait statistics information for all the operations in the database level. This DMV can be utilized to diagnose performance issues with the database and other query execution.

- `sys.dm_database_copies`. Provides information about the geo-replication copies for the database. Details like `maximum_lag` and `replication_state_desc` can be used to determine the latency and status of replication.

Execution Related Information

Most of the execution related DMVs available with Microsoft SQL Server are also available with Azure SQL Databases and can be used to determine the performance issues, execution related issues, etc. The following are some of the commonly used DMVs:

- `sys.dm_exec_requests/sys.dm_exec_sessions/sys.dm_exec_connections`. Provides information about the sessions connected to (or active requests executing on) the Azure SQL Database.

- `sys.dm_exec_query_stats, sys.dm_exec_function_stats,sys.dm_exec_procedure_stats, sys.dm_exec_trigger_stats`. Provide aggregated execution statistics for queries, procedures, functions, and triggers, respectively. These DMVs can be utilized to determine the top duration/CPU consuming/read/write queries executing on the server. Entries from these DMVs are removed when the corresponding queries or objects are removed from the cache.

- `sys.dm_exec_query_memory_grants`. Provides information about memory grants (pending or granted) for each query running on the database.

Other DMVs are available with Azure SQL Database to monitor various details like database indexes, security of the database or the logical server, etc. A complete list of all the DMVs is available on MSDN.

Using Extended Events

Extended Events or (XEvents) are not new. They have been available with Microsoft SQL Server since the SQL Server 2008 days. There has been a lot of optimization and improvements done to this feature over the last several years. The amount of information available through XEvents is enormous, which can be determined by the fact that the upcoming release of SQL Server, SQL Server 2016, has almost 1,200 events exposed.

Extended Events available on Azure SQL Database is only a subset of the feature available with SQL Server. These extended events are scoped to a single Azure SQL database, meaning that an extended event running against one Azure SQL database cannot be used to monitor events against another database on the same logical server.

Listing 10-2 provides a sample script that can be used to determine the events/actions available with Extended Events on Azure SQL Database.

Listing 10-2. T-SQL Script to Determine the Events or Actions Available with Azure SQL Database

```
SELECT
        o.object_type,
        p.name          AS [package_name],
        o.name          AS [db_object_name],
        o.description   AS [db_obj_description]
FROM
                    sys.dm_xe_objects AS o
        INNER JOIN sys.dm_xe_packages AS p  ON p.guid = o.package_guid
WHERE
        o.object_type in
            (
            'event','action'
            )
ORDER BY
        o.object_type,
        p.name,
        o.name;
```

The easiest way to configure Extended Events for Azure SQL Database is to use SQL Server Management Studio, as illustrated in Figure 10-13. In SSMs, Extended Events can be accessed by expanding the database node.

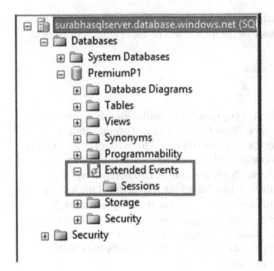

Figure 10-13. *Accessing Extended Events*

A new session can be configured by right-clicking on the session node and choosing either New Session Wizard or New Session. Either of the options are fairly straightforward to use.

Following is a sample T-SQL script to create an XEvent to monitor blocking and deadlock:

```
CREATE EVENT SESSION [Sample_XEvents] ON DATABASE

ADD EVENT sqlos.wait_info(
    ACTION(sqlserver.database_name,sqlserver.session_id,sqlserver.sql_text)),
ADD EVENT sqlserver.blocked_process_report(
    ACTION(sqlserver.database_name,sqlserver.session_id,sqlserver.sql_text)),
ADD EVENT sqlserver.database_xml:deadlock_report(
    ACTION(sqlserver.database_name,sqlserver.session_id,sqlserver.sql_text)),
ADD EVENT sqlserver.lock_deadlock(
    ACTION(sqlserver.database_name,sqlserver.session_id,sqlserver.sql_text)),
ADD EVENT sqlserver.sp_statement_completed(
    ACTION(sqlserver.database_name,sqlserver.session_id,sqlserver.sql_text)),
ADD EVENT sqlserver.sql_batch_completed(
    ACTION(sqlserver.database_name,sqlserver.session_id,sqlserver.sql_text))

ADD TARGET package0.event_file(
            SET filename=N'https://YourStorageAccountName.blob.core.
            windows.net/ContainerName/OutputFile.xel'),
ADD TARGET package0.ring_buffer

WITH (STARTUP_STATE=ON)
GO
```

Similar sessions can be created to monitor other events on the SQL Database.

Control permission is required to create an Extended Events. This permission is available by default to the DBO user.

Information about currently running XEvent sessions and other information regarding the events, actions, targets, etc. exposed through XEvents can be derived from the several DMVs and catalog views exposed by Azure SQL Database. Following are some of the most commonly used DMVs and catalog views:

- sys.dm_xe_database_session_events. Exposes information about the events configured for the currently active sessions.

- sys.dm_xe_database_sessions. Exposes information about the currently active Extended Event sessions.

- sys.database_event_sessions. Exposes information about all the XEvents sessions configured on the SQL database.

- sys.dm_xe_objects. Provides information about the events, actions, targets, etc. exposed by XEvents on Azure SQL Database. This DMV is similar to the one available with Microsoft SQL Server.

Extended Events can be useful in determining performance issues or other issues with the Azure SQL Database. But take care not to overload the database with too many sessions or events being captured. Doing so can cause over-committing memory and ultimately lead to database performance issues.

Summary

This chapter discussed the Database Throughput Unit (DTU) and how choosing the right performance level is of paramount importance. We discussed how the services tier and the performance level of an Azure SQL database can be changed and then talked about the various performance optimization and monitoring features available with Azure SQL Database and on the Azure Management Portal.

Index

Get the eBook for only $5!

Why limit yourself?

Now you can take the weightless companion with you wherever you go and access your content on your PC, phone, tablet, or reader.

Since you've purchased this print book, we're happy to offer you the eBook in all 3 formats for just $5.

Convenient and fully searchable, the PDF version enables you to easily find and copy code—or perform examples by quickly toggling between instructions and applications. The MOBI format is ideal for your Kindle, while the ePUB can be utilized on a variety of mobile devices.

To learn more, go to www.apress.com/companion or contact support@apress.com.

Printed in the United States
By Bookmasters